Praise for Bruce Morrill's

Encountering Christ in the Eucharist

"The author's rare combination of writing with theological insight and pastoral experience makes this book highly accessible to a wide audience. It deserves to be used in the college classroom as well as in ongoing formation programs for adult Christians."
—*Kevin W. Irwin, professor of liturgical studies and sacramental theology, Catholic University of America*

"Bruce Morrill's work is firmly rooted in the Roman Catholic tradition and yet imbued with a sense of ecumenicity that allows for many conversations to unfold. I will be using this book in my classes in liturgical studies, which are attended by a wide range of students from different Christian traditions. Especially for Protestants who seek to find a renewed point of entrance into sacramental theology, the reflections on sacraments as encounters with the living Christ in which grace as event unfolds are helpful."
—*Andrea Bieler, professor of Christian worship, Pacific School of Religion, Berkeley*

"It is rare to find an interpretation of the Eucharist that is brilliantly and creatively responsible to a particular ecclesial tradition, in this case the Roman Catholic tradition, and at the same time ecumenically informed, helpful, and wise. Bruce Morrill has given us exactly such a book. Beginning wonderfully with the gathered assembly as the fundamental symbol of the risen Christ, Morrill interprets the whole liturgical flow of word and table as forming us in the Spirit of the crucified risen one to turn in service toward God's beloved world. On the way, he richly illuminates the presence of Christ in the word and the troubled but irreplaceable metaphor *sacrifice*. And when one is done reading his lucid text, one comes again into the eucharistic assembly with new depth of insight." —*Gordon W. Lathrop, professor of liturgy emeritus, Lutheran Theological Seminary at Philadelphia*

"The Eucharist is a unified mystery whose light is reflected off different facets, each of which is a dimension of one single integrated mystery, and we must walk around the mystery to catch its brilliant flashes. Bruce Morrill seeks out the multidimensional symbol ritual of the Eucharist in a way that sees the interconnectedness of each element. Christ is hidden, yet Christ comes, he abides, and he leads his people. This fourfold structure brings Morrill to discuss, in turn, the baptized, the word of God in Scripture, sacramental food and drink, and the Church's ministers. By keeping his eye on the unifying mystery behind these facets of our eucharistic celebration, Morrill attempts to reconcile approaches that have been unfortunately polarized: individual and communal, lay and cleric, spirituality and social action, transcendent and immanent. Through placing these facets of the Eucharist in synthesis, Morrill has refreshed traditional categories of our faith for our understanding." —*David W. Fagerberg, associate professor of theology, University of Notre Dame*

"As we have come to expect from Bruce Morrill, this is a well-wrought book, accessible and brief enough to serve in an introductory course on the sacraments, yet thorough and constructive enough to serve as a capstone for a graduate seminar. Though its focus is on the Eucharist, it is more fully a theology of sacrament, uniting Word, words, symbol, and community. Morrill leads us safely through some of the theological minefields of the church's sacramental history, bringing us, finally, to a sacramental theology that will be of pastoral use to Protestants and Roman Catholics alike." —*E. Byron Anderson, Styberg Professor of Worship, Garrett-Evangelical Theological Seminary*

Encountering Christ in the Eucharist

The Paschal Mystery in People, Word, and Sacrament

BRUCE T. MORRILL, SJ

Paulist Press
New York / Mahwah, NJ

Cover and book design by Lynn Else
Cover Image: Photographer IngridHS/iStockphoto.com

Library of Congress Cataloging-in-Publication Data

Morrill, Bruce T.
    Encountering Christ in the Eucharist : the Paschal mystery in people, word, and sacrament / Bruce T. Morrill.
      p. cm.
    Includes bibliographical references (p.   ) and index.
    ISBN 978-0-8091-4768-7 (alk. paper) — ISBN 978-1-61643-141-9 1. Lord's Supper—Real presence. 2. Mass. I. Title.
    BV825.3.M67 2012
    234`.163—dc23

                                      2011049060

Published by Paulist Press
997 Macarthur Boulevard
Mahwah, New Jersey 07430

www.paulistpress.com

Printed and bound in the
United States of America

Contents

Contents

Acknowledgments

I present this book with an ecumenical spirit and in hope that it might serve in some small way the church's great work of celebrating the Eucharist. Portions of material in two of these chapters first appeared, in different forms, in articles I published in the journal *Liturgical Ministry*. My thanks to Sister Joyce Ann Zimmerman, CPPS, editor, for her affirming my use of that material. My Jesuit confrere John Baldovin has my gratitude for expertly reviewing the draft of chapter 4. I am likewise grateful to the Philadelphia area members of the North American Academy of Liturgy who, at the invitation of Tim Brunk and under the leadership of Larry Sibley, gave me feedback on chapter 3 during their semi-annual meeting in the fall of 2010. Gail Ramshaw was particularly helpful concerning the Revised Common Lectionary. In addition, the manuscript benefited from an entire read by several colleagues and friends: Austin Campbell generously read it with a view to its accessibility for a general educated audience. Andrea Bieler graciously highlighted certain aspects of the text, while Ron Anderson combed the pages with his critical editor's eye to detail. Gordon Lathrop humbled me with extensive comments delivered verbally with warm encouragement and on paper in his microfine handwriting! Any shortcomings in the text, nonetheless, are entirely the responsibility of the author.

Bruce T. Morrill, SJ

Introduction

Participating in the Mystery of Christ's Sacramental Presence

Mystery: Revelation of God's Saving Love for Humanity

The Eucharist is God's fundamental gift to the church—as a body and in each of its members—whereby we come to know ourselves over and again, at times even more deeply and intimately, as sharing in the very life and mission of Christ Jesus and his Spirit. To reflect theologically on the church's traditional practice of the Eucharist is to delve into mystery—indeed, the mystery at the heart of Christian faith and the life of the church.

The word *mystery* here is not meant to hinder believers' use of reason and imagination as they seek a greater appreciation and joy in celebrating the Eucharist. Rather, to speak of the Eucharist as mystery is to acknowledge at the outset the complexity of our inquiry, and this not as a forbidding caution but a promising invitation. In fact, "mystery" was the preferred term of the earliest Christians for referring not only to the Eucharist and baptism but to all the concrete ways in which they experienced God entering into and shaping their lives in Christ.

The Greek word *mystèrion* occurs repeatedly in the New Testament, drawing upon Jewish biblical tradition wherein God's knowledge is hidden, secret, beyond human comprehension, yet needed to solve earthly difficulties. The range of literature in the Hebrew scriptures unfolds numerous ways that God reveals God's

1

plans, purpose, and wisdom to the people; these ways include the law, words of the prophets, intermediaries such as angels, and visions. At times the divine mysteries, even when revealed, are too much for human comprehension, setting up a trajectory through the prophetic and apocalyptic literature toward a fullness of revelation to come at the end of the ages. The first believers in Jesus as the Christ and Son of God believed that in him the dawn of the final age had come. Thus, it is not surprising to find the New Testament authors regularly employing the language of mystery in reference not only to the gift of faith or the revelation of the kingdom but also to such inscrutable wisdom as the already/not yet tension of salvation in Christ or the incomprehensibility of the general resurrection (for example, Rom 11:25; 1 Cor 15:51).

In scripture and tradition, then, mysteries are about the revelation of divine wisdom as the fullness of life for the world (see 1 Cor 2:6–8), God's invitation into the seemingly unapproachable light piercing through the events of history. The gift of faith in Christ discloses Jesus—his person, mission, suffering, death, and glorification—as the fullness of revelation. Christ Jesus is not only the message but also the means, through the gift of the Holy Spirit, of sharing in the sure purpose of God for humans. Still, God remains God, the Lord of heaven and earth, whose ways are not our ways (see Isa 55:8), the holy one so different from us humans in perfect justice and love as to give us in Christ a peace we cannot give ourselves (see John 14:27). Believers live by faith in the God who in Jesus showed himself utterly committed to the thriving of people in this good but fallen creation, by hope in the promises hidden in fragmentary moments of life and by a love that in Christlike attitude and deeds draws us into his way as the very truth of life itself.

Celebrating the Liturgy:
Participation in Christ's Paschal Mystery

Over the past century sacramental and liturgical theology has undergone a theoretical reformation and advanced a renewal in liturgical practice by identifying and adopting a concept of central importance to early church tradition: When Christians assemble for divine worship we, the church, participate in the reality of the *paschal mystery*, that is, in Christ's passion, death, resurrection, and conferral of the Holy Spirit. To celebrate the liturgy is to share in the very life of God revealed in the saving deeds of Jesus, whose death and resurrection during the annual paschal (Passover) feast disclosed the meaning of all the acts of his mission that culminated in that ultimate mystery. The distinctive Christian belief in God as Trinity is founded upon an experiential knowing of God in and through the person of Jesus; thus, the early church fathers came to write of Jesus himself as the mystery of God. Jesus is the revelation of the trinitarian God of love.

The importance of recovering this ancient concept of the paschal mystery, French sacramental theologian Louis-Marie Chauvet argues, lies in locating and celebrating the source of salvation, as the New Testament does, in Jesus' death and resurrection. Chauvet emphasizes this in contrast to the classical scholastic theology of the sacraments, which took the incarnation as its starting point, focusing on the question of how the divine Word could take on and sanctify human, created reality. The sacraments thereby came to be understood as "the prolongation of the redeeming incarnation," the liturgy as celebrating "the various 'anniversaries' of Jesus' destiny," and the church year as "a sort of immense sociodrama in which one would somehow mime the events that have punctuated this destiny."[1] Attendance at liturgy became a matter of watching the *completed* drama of Christ's life rather than entering into and thus *sharing in* the mystery of the Father's call and the Spirit's empowerment of Jesus for a self-emptying mission of service even unto death, but finally into life.[2] The latter is a dynamic

3

saving process that, while definitively inaugurated in Jesus' Passover, has yet to reach its final completion in "a new heaven and a new earth" (2 Pet 3:13; Rev 21:1). Recognizing the vitality of that eschatological tension at the heart of the church's life and work, Russian Orthodox theologian Alexander Schmemann came to describe its liturgy as "an all-embracing vision of life, a power meant to judge, inform and transform the whole of existence, a 'philosophy of life' shaping and challenging all our ideas, attitudes and actions...an *icon* of that new life which is to challenge and renew the 'old life' in us and around us."[3] Such is the fundamentally eschatological nature of the mystery of Christian faith and thus of the liturgy as the lived knowledge of that faith.

Eschatology is, indeed, about the "last things" and "end of the age," but these not as something only to be imagined (dreadfully or otherwise) in the future but rather as already inaugurated in Jesus' resurrection yet awaiting completion in his second coming. This time "in between," living by faith in the "already" of Jesus' resurrection and the "not yet" of the ongoing history of the world's suffering, is the eschatological time of the church. We, the baptized, live this eschatological reality in the history of our time, not only for our individual salvation, not merely for our personal piety, but for the sake of a world still so often bent on rejecting the just and merciful ways of God's Christ. What sustains the church and its members as the Body of Christ now sharing in God's life for the world is the Eucharist, the sacrifice of praise and thanksgiving joining our lives to his, empowering us to be, as St. Augustine taught, what we place upon and receive from the altar.[4]

Ecumenical theologian Jean-Marie-Roger Tillard's writings bid us turn again to the New Testament to learn that we, the church, comprise "a spiritual house" built of "living stones," ourselves engaged daily in "spiritual sacrifices" (1 Pet 2:5) that glorify God by building up the goodness of humanity (see also, Rom 12:1; Heb 10:19–25). Contrary to the modern expectation that such a term would refer to sacred rituals, the term *spiritual sacrifices* in the earliest Christian writings (biblical and patristic) refers to believers' ongoing offering of their very lives in service to others. What makes such a life of virtues practiced in service to others, especially the poor, *holy* is the larger reality wherein Christians pursue it, namely, a sharing in the life and death of the Jesus who has become the final (eschatological) revelation of God. The church shares in its members the deep, abiding knowledge of the mystery of God as self-emptying love for humanity in celebrating the Eucharist: "In the Eucharist, the sacrifice of Christ and the 'spiritual sacrifice' of the church become one because Christ takes the members of his Body into the embrace of his sacrifice."[5] Thus, the eschatological nature of the liturgy carries an irreducible ethical and social imperative, our own call to know Christ by following him in words and deeds, participating in the reign of God that has come in him, the one who will come again. But to so live in Christ we need to know him, not merely to know about him or his teaching, but to know him intimately in a deep bond of friendship (see John 15:15).[6] So that we may know him now, to "have the words of eternal life" (John 6:68) written on our bodies in this time between his first and second comings, in this time of the church, Jesus left us the Eucharist as the sacrificial meal in which we share in his paschal mystery.

Renewing Liturgical Tradition: Life for the Church, Life for the World

As is the case with any person, Jesus becomes known to his followers by what he says and does and by sharing with them the memories that have established and continue to advance this most important of friendships. The Spirit of the risen Christ imparts the saving, life-giving mystery of those memories to the Body of his church in the narrative word of scripture, made effectively present through the ritual gestures of sacramental liturgy, and existentially appropriated through ethical lives characterized by justice and mercy, forgiveness and compassion. Historically,

different traditions within the one church of Christ have empha-
sized different aspects or even the entire reality of this most fundamental mystery of the faith, resulting in a richness of diversity
that nonetheless lent itself to distortions within the practices of
the traditions themselves.

Eastern Orthodoxy has always thought of the mystical heart
of the Divine Liturgy, celebrated strictly on Sunday and a few
other major feasts, in terms of ascending into the perichoretic
(mutually shared or interpenetrating) love of the Trinity.
Orthodoxy developed extensive normative elements for the worship space—the layout and decoration of the church interior, the
choreography of movements and style of music, and so forth—
meant to raise participants into the heavenly banquet of the kingdom of God. The problem, however, is that such elaborate symbolism collapsed under its weight into fragments: popular piety
developed hybrid meanings for individual symbolic elements
(processions, gestures, vestments) in isolation from their function
within the liturgy as a whole.[7]

As for the West, while Luther and Calvin recognized the primordial importance for the church of celebrating the Eucharist on
the Lord's Day, the subsequent evolution across much of
Protestantism and Anglicanism, often in polemical environments,
saw a marginalization of the Lord's Supper to occasional enact-
ments during the year. The preferred Protestant language of Lord's
Supper, symbolizing the biblical warrant for the ritual action (see
Luke 22:19; 1 Cor 11:25), highlights the authority of the word of
God in scripture over traditions of Eucharist or Mass. One can generally say that for Protestants, worship on Sunday became centered
on the proclamation of the biblical word through the reading of
scripture, preaching, hymnody, and prayers.[8] Roman Catholic sacramental practice and theology, however, during the medieval era and
then all the stronger in the Catholic Reformation, developed an all-
but-exclusive focus on the descent of Christ to the altar, the site of
his real presence in the host. That the Latin term *hostia* means "victim," understood as Christ's body sacrificed on the cross, is indica-

tive of how narrowly the Roman Catholic understanding and practice of the Eucharist became focused on worshiping the "sacred species" of Christ's body in the sacrament.

In the early twentieth century the impetus for reform and renewal of the liturgy emerged in Benedictine abbeys in Belgium and Germany in what became known as the Liturgical Movement. Historical and pastoral initiatives complemented scholarly theological work in monasteries and theological faculties in a number of European countries and, eventually, North America. The movement realized steady ecumenical and official impact, evidenced in the 1950s by Pope Pius XII's encyclical *Mediator Dei* and the Church of England's establishing its Liturgical Commission, and still later, *Baptism, Eucharist and Ministry*, the 1982 Faith and Order paper of the World Council of Churches. The climax, nonetheless, came with the Second Vatican Council's *Sacrosanctum Concilium*, the 1963 Constitution on the Sacred Liturgy. This document not only promulgated reform of the Roman ritual but was also widely embraced by Protestants and Anglicans in their efforts at liturgical renewal.

Key principles of the constitution include identifying the liturgy as the source and summit of the church's entire life (no. 10) and, therefore, the full and active participation by all the people as the highest priority for realizing the pastoral, humanly sanctifying potential of the liturgy (no. 14). As a corrective to the practical equation of worship with gazing at the sacrificial victim in the host, the council fathers recovered the "sound tradition" (no. 4) of liturgy as ritual activity singularly capable of nourishing the faith lives of all through the full complement of its symbols, actions, and words.

> For in the liturgy God speaks to His people and Christ is still proclaiming His gospel. And the people reply to God both by song and prayer.
>
> Moreover, the prayers addressed to God by the priest who presides over the assembly in the person of Christ are said in the name of the entire holy people and of all

present. And the visible signs used by the liturgy to signify invisible divine things have been chosen by Christ
or the Church. Thus not only when things are read
"which were written for our instruction" (Rom. 15:4),
but also when the Church prays or sings or acts, the
faith of those taking part is nourished and their minds
are raised to God, so that they may offer Him their
rational service and more abundantly receive His
grace....[9]

Celebration of the full range of words, symbols, and gestures in
the liturgy disposes the faithful to receive the graces of drawing
close to God in worship and gaining strength for practicing charity (no. 59). The council's teaching amounts to a splendid renewal
of the ancient relationship between the liturgical assembly's sacrifice of thankful praise and the myriad spiritual sacrifices its
members perform in their daily lives. "In doing this," writes
Irénée Henri Dalmais, "the Church pursues its most essential purpose, which is to ensure the active presence of divine realties
under the conditions of our present life—and that is precisely
what 'mystery' means."[10]

Encountering Christ in the Eucharistic Celebration

The active presence of divine realities in the human work of
liturgy is nothing other than another way to speak of mystery. And
the mystery, as we have seen, is Christ Jesus himself. To celebrate
the paschal mystery is to encounter the presence of a living person: Jesus the Christ, sharing himself with his sisters and broth-
ers. Such intimate sharing in human friendship between the Lord,
who has ascended bodily to the right hand of his heavenly Father,
and earthly people comes through the divine power of the Spirit
working through the ritual's human words and symbols. Christ
relates to the earthly members of his Body precisely in our bodily

means of mutual presence and receptivity, that is, *sacramentally*, in the liturgy, touching senses and memory, intellect and emotion, to form us as his members. Just as the flourishing of human friendship requires multiple modes of symbolic communication, one person to the other, so the risen Lord's sacramental presence to the faithful comes through a number of distinct yet interrelated modes. Thus does the Constitution on the Sacred Liturgy teach that Christ accomplishes "so great a work" by being present in the assembled people as they pray and sing, in the person of the presiding minister, in the proclamation of the word, and in the sacraments, "especially under the Eucharistic species."[11] Here the distortions and old polemics giving precedence to one means of grace to the exclusion of others—for example, preaching of the word versus adoring the consecrated host—fall away to the oblivion they deserve. For if the Word incarnate is to take ever-fuller form in us, then the divine Spirit who raised him from the dead (Rom 8:11) must work with all dimensions of our ritual bodies so that we might share in his saving work.

Far from being a modern innovation in eucharistic theology, the council's teaching of Christ's presence in the gathered people, presiding minister, proclaimed word, and the blessed bread and cup, broken and shared, comes as an evangelical call to renew our practice and reflection upon this most precious gift for the church. The Gospel of Luke unfolds the elements of the liturgy in the engrossing narrative of the road to Emmaus (24:13–35).[12] The story takes place on the Lord's Day, Sunday, the very day of Christ's resurrection, with Jesus mysteriously joining two of his disciples as they walk home from the disaster of his execution during the paschal (Passover) festival in Jerusalem. The two disciples symbolize the church, whose members find their way enlightened by the Christ who takes charge of their conversation, presiding over their sharing and revealing the hidden wisdom of his paschal suffering by opening anew, as if for the first time, the scriptures. The disciples respond to the Lord's proclamation of the word by inviting him to table, where the full, redeeming force of the paschal mystery climactically comes home to them when he takes, blesses, breaks, and shares the bread.

True to the mysterious nature of divine–human encounter, Luke's account of the presence of the risen Jesus has a hidden quality throughout, but with a paradoxical twist: as the disciples come to recognize him in the breaking of the bread, they realize more fully the implications of the biblical word he had broken open for them *as the very mystery come now to life in them.* In light of the sacramental action, the full force of the word the Lord had proclaimed in their company sets their hearts blazing and their feet back on the road. Only now, however, they hit the road with purpose, the mission of bringing the message of Christ crucified to life for the world.

Luke's story of Jesus and the disciples "on the way"[13] to Emmaus reflects the earliest believers' liturgical experience of the risen Christ, an experience that itself followed the pattern of divine presence they and Jesus knew in their Jewish tradition. Peter Fink identifies and explains these several distinct yet related modes of signified divine presence and how the first believers experienced them anew in the person of Christ:

> The Jews knew a fourfold experience of the presence of God, and drew up a set of stories and symbols to identify each shade of that fourfold experience. God was the God who *comes*, on his own initiative and at his own time. God was likewise the God who *leads*, who goes before, who prepares the way. God was also the God who *abides*, dwelling freely among his people. And God was the God who *hides*, with the primary mask of the hidden God being the people themselves. In the experience of the Risen One the early Christians named Jesus Christ in exactly the same way. He is the Christ who *comes* ("Maranatha"), the Christ who *leads* ("I go before you"), the Christ who *abides* ("I am with you all

days"), and the Christ who *hides* ("You are the body of Christ").[14]

That primordial sacramental experience of the risen Christ grounds the church's liturgical experience of Christ's presence: "In word Christ comes; in presider Christ leads; in food Christ abides; in assembly Christ lives hidden."[15]

Historically, the church has struggled in theology and practice to hold in dynamic tension the transcendent images of Christ's coming and hiding, which symbolize an illusive divine power beyond human control, with the immanent images of Christ's leading and abiding, which symbolize tangible human access to God in the sacraments. As Fink observes, "The transcendent images alone threaten to lose Christ in otherness; the immanent images alone threaten to bring Christ under human control."[16] The danger lies in suppressing either the immanent or transcendent dimensions—the failure either to recognize the humbling revelation of Christ's actual presence in one's fellow believers or, conversely, to perceive that through ministry of word and sacrament the assembled people are being led into the very mystery of God. The Spirit of the risen Christ nourishes the members of his body, the church, in the Eucharist through the dynamic interplay of all four symbolic modes of his presence that, as in the Easter story of Emmaus, reach their climax in the sharing of his body and blood in the form of sacramental mystery.

The following four chapters explore the multidimensional symbolic ritual of the Eucharist in order to understand how the faithful thereby receive the revelation of God in Christ so as to embody the Spirit-life of the crucified and risen Jesus in the world. We begin with the presence of *Christ hidden* in the faithful, the baptized who have been sealed in the Spirit of Christ for lives of worship that come to light when assembled at the table of the word and Eucharist. Here biblical traditions of covenant, blood, and spirit figure in understanding the meaning of the central symbols that inform the Christian liturgical assembly. Chapter 2 is devoted to how *Christ comes* through the proclaimed word of God in scripture, with each liturgy comprising an original event of revelation for participants that is shaped, nonetheless, by the paschal imagination of the church year's order of readings. That imagination acquires concrete form in the members of the assembled body as they move from the service of the word to the Eucharist, where *Christ abides* in sacramental food and drink as the medium for a real sharing in the very life of God. Through special attention to the tradition's source in the Gospel of John, chapter 3 articulates how the sacrificial meal enacts the mutual presence of persons, divine and human, one to another, to nourish a love stronger than death. Finally, chapter 4 considers how *Christ leads* his people through those who minister to word and sacrament in the church.

In the course of our exploration of the Eucharist we shall discover both the immanence (closeness) and transcendence (otherness) of the God we worship. Unfolding the immanent (leading, abiding) and transcendent (coming, hiding) dimensions of the divine presence in the liturgy can help us appreciate the humbling revelation of the Spirit of Christ's presence and action in our fellow believers, church, and world as well as increase our awareness that through word and sacrament we are being led into the very mystery of God.

Chapter One

Hidden Presence

The Mystery of the Assembly as Body of Christ

The Assembly of the Baptized

"Liturgical services pertain to the whole body of the Church; they manifest it and have effects upon it."[1] Here the entire theology of the church as sacrament, along with the theology of the church's sacraments, springs to life, inviting reflection on how the eucharistic liturgy nurtures the People of God's mission of witnessing to the Gospel hidden in their midst.

Conceiving of the church as sacrament of Christ, a theological move initiated some decades ago and officially endorsed at Vatican II, is, as Bernard Cooke has observed, a recent and "almost revolutionary" change in ecclesial thought and practice.[2] The shift, still only slowly being realized, is from an individualistic "receiving" of sacraments to a communal sharing in the sacramental life of the church as the People of God, the living and active signs of God's salvific will for the world as definitively revealed in Christ. The scandal of the cross has passed over into the scandal of the church, that is, into the stupefying claim that in such ordinary, limited, and sinful people as ourselves God is revealing God's unbounded love, mercy, and forgiveness for the world. The way in which we are able thus to know and believe in ourselves and the fate of our world is through the ritual sacraments of the church, wherein the sacramentality of the church's members and all cre-

13   *Gospel hidden.*

ation is manifested by means of the symbols, words, and gestures the church has come to designate as its sacraments.

Although recent and revolutionary, however, such a theology of church and sacraments is not new but, rather, a recovery of the ecclesiologies of the New Testament and the formative first centuries of Christianity. While we currently tend to symbolize this eucharistically grounded communion-reality of the church in St. Paul's image of the Body of Christ, this ecclesial view actually pervades the books of the New Testament: "One is saved only by being 'in Christ and his Spirit' [1 John]; one is 'in Christ' only by being a member of the body [1 Corinthians], a branch of the vine [John], a living stone of the 'priestly house' [1 Peter], a believer active in the charity of 'works' [James]; one is all this in solidarity with others."[3] The Holy Spirit binds individuals into this communion through baptism, while leading this communion toward perfection in the Eucharist. Thus, baptism in water and the Holy Spirit is intimately connected to Eucharist as the body and blood of Christ. Indeed, the latter is only possible if the former continuously takes place. Without the presence of living members, the church cannot be the communion it is called to be in history and empowered to share through the eucharistic liturgy.

At its origins in the New Testament, Christian initiation is fundamentally about God's gracious redemption of people through their entrance into the Spirit-life of the crucified and risen Christ shared in the church. Not only is the entire process of Christian initiation the gift and work of the Holy Spirit, the Spirit is present and active in the ongoing growth in faith (the sanctification) of each Christian life as well as in the building up of the entire People of God. From this, two crucial points must be noted: first, Christian initiation is never completed in this life but, rather, sets believers into a mysterious participation in the very life of the triune God that will only be fully known after our bodily resurrection from the dead (see Rom 6:1–12). For this reason, the theory and practice of Christian initiation can never be simply reduced to anthropological and psychological models of human

14

[handwritten margin note: So we are present in our connectedness and in individual persons —]

passage and development, even though our ongoing sanctification and salvation is being worked out by the Spirit's grace in the very processes of our human lives. This means that, second, the gift and work of the Holy Spirit cannot be isolated or restricted to any one moment or action in the life of believers or the church as a whole (that is, the Body of Christ), even though the triune God manifests or reveals the promise and gift of the Spirit's life not only for believers but for the entire world in the sacramental liturgy of the church. But this is the very purpose of Christian liturgy (*leitourgia*), namely, the glorifying of God through the sanctification of people. The Spirit animates *all* this work.

Baptism and Eucharist are the primary sacraments of the church. As the General Introduction to Christian Initiation in the reformed Roman Rite teaches, baptism "rescues us from the power of darkness, and brings us to the dignity of adopted children, a new creation through water and the Holy Spirit."[4] The Holy Spirit, the very power of love shared within the persons of God, is also the power of God poured out in creating the world in its fundamental goodness and redeeming it in its fallen condition.[5] For this reason baptism entails an invocation, signing, and washing in the name of the Trinity; it brings believers into communion with—that is, gives them a participatory sharing in the very life of—the Father, Son, and Holy Spirit. Thus does the World Council of Churches, in its *Baptism, Eucharist and Ministry*, state:

> Administered in obedience to our Lord, baptism is a sign and seal of our common discipleship. Through baptism, Christians are brought into union with Christ, with each other and with the Church of every time and place....Baptism initiates the reality of the new life given in the midst of the present world. It gives participation in the community of the Holy Spirit.[6]

Baptism is primary to the church and among the sacraments in its once-for-all, momentous function of bringing all Christians into new existence as daughters and sons of God in Christ, empowering them with his Spirit for lives witnessing together to the kingdom of God.

The Eucharist is the other primary sacrament insofar as it functions as the source and summit[7] of the ongoing lives of believers, of the church in history: *"Baptism needs to be constantly reaffirmed. The most obvious form of such reaffirmation is the celebration of the eucharist."*[8] Assembling on the Lord's Day, the original Christian feast that fashions the church's passage through time, believers perceive anew their communal identity as the Body of Christ by sharing in his eucharistic body and blood. It is the Holy Spirit, invoked upon both the gifts and assembly during the eucharistic prayer, who transforms all as communion in the divine life revealed in the Crucified. Nor does the calling down of the Spirit's gifts end there. Anticipating the heavenly banquet, "we pray for a greater outpouring of the Holy Spirit, so that the whole human race may be brought into the unity of God's family."[9] Thus does the church repeatedly call upon the gift of the Spirit, and thus does the Spirit animate the primary sacramental liturgy of the church for its mission in service to the world.

The mystery, the elusiveness, the hidden quality of this profound reality of ecclesial faith was no less problematic for the earliest communities than for Christians today. Perhaps the most notorious case is the socioeconomic divisions of the Sunday assembly of the church in Corinth, whom Paul had to admonish and, in so doing, instruct on the corporate reality of their sharing in the eucharistic body of Christ.[10] The challenge of realizing the mystery that our redemption comes through our sharing life as God's people motivated, in no small part, the writing of the letters attributed to Paul, Peter, James, and John. Exemplary is J.-M.-R. Tillard's commentary on 1 Peter, a baptismal instruction on mutual love and service as constituting the spiritual sacrifices (*pneumatikai thusiai*) whereby believers worship God:

These sacrifices are not primarily liturgical cultic actions but the existential acts of the holy life of this commu-

16

nity. Its communion comes fundamentally from the Spirit, and it serves God in the daily actions of its members....To become holy "in all [one's] conduct" (1:15) means to place oneself, with faith and courage, within the network of relationships based on baptism which together make of the community, not a collection of persons seeking their own sanctification, but the unique and indivisible "royal priesthood," the "priestly community of the king," the "spiritual house" of God. In the holiness of all those whom the gospel has engendered "anew" (1:23; see 2:2), individual and community cannot be separated....The individual is a living stone of the "spiritual house" (2:5) only by remaining bonded to others and acting with the awareness of this bond.[11]

This same sort of challenge motivates the contemporary need to appreciate the sacraments, and paradigmatically the Eucharist, as the fundamental means whereby the church shares its common life in the Spirit of Christ and comes to know itself as the body through whom Christ now explicitly lives and acts for the salvation of the world.

The way the early church eventually came to assurance of the presence of the Spirit of Christ within the members of its liturgical body was through the concept of sacramental character. This is perhaps an initially off-putting philosophical concept. A brief historical review of this notion of character may nonetheless prove theologically helpful for understanding the liturgically assembled church as a real-symbolic presence of the crucified and risen Lord. When biblically grounded and corporately understood, sacramental character is a traditional notion conveying the divine initiative and ecclesial claim on the members of the eucharistic assembly. Those divine and ecclesial characteristics, moreover, are at the biblical heart of the status and mission of the liturgical assembly itself, specifically through Christ's appropriation of the covenant tradition of his people, Israel. Exploration of character, covenant, and assembly, then, comprises the work of the next two sections of this chapter.

Sacramental Character: Sealed in the Spirit for Lives of Worship

The metaphorical notion of a seal permanently affixed to each new member of the Body of Christ emerged early in the history of theological reflection on the sacrament of baptism. In various letters and treatises the fathers of the church sought to understand the mystery of salvation that they and their Christian communities were experiencing. With a deep faith in the presence of God's Spirit in the church and in the authenticity of the church's tradition based on its apostolic origins, the fathers considered the ritual practices of their churches as theological data, as concrete expressions of the true faith. The fathers came to reflect upon certain facts about the church's sacramental actions that, in turn, led to theories about the sacraments. This reflection they performed with the use of two other theological resources: sacred scripture and Greek philosophy.

The Latin fathers searched the scriptures to understand how it is that a person is "sealed with the Spirit" in the ritual of baptism. Probing the images of sealing and anointing in both the Old and New Testaments, they came to associate the concept of sacramental seal with a notion found in the letters of St. Paul, the *sphragis* (seal) of the Holy Spirit: "But it is God who establishes us with you in Christ and has anointed us, by putting his seal on us and giving us his Spirit in our hearts as a first installment" (2 Cor 1:21–22). The fathers correlated this scriptural metaphor of being sealed with the Spirit with images from Greco-Roman society, the permanent and indelible brands or tattoos on soldiers and slaves or the wax seal on a letter bearing the impress of a person's signet ring. Moreover, by a certain philosophical reading of the Gospel and Letters of John, they came to understand the concept of this seal or character (the Latin term) not simply as a metaphor but as a metaphysical reality. Rather than being a physical sign marking the surface of the body, the seal of the Holy Spirit was an invisible character impressed on the soul.

A theologically rigorous concept of sacramental character emerged in the teaching of Augustine, bishop of Hippo, who in opposition to the Donatists developed the notion of the *dominicus character* as the "indelible quality" that results from sacramental incorporation in the church.[12] Over the course of the fourth century the common belief that baptism (as well as priestly ordination) was unrepeatable became a contested issue. Donatus and other North African bishops rejected the decision of the Council of Arles (314) that people baptized by clergy who had renounced the faith during persecutions need not be rebaptized, nor did those ordained by defecting bishops need a second ordination. In the early fifth century Augustine addressed the problem with a precision of terminology. Augustine reasoned that baptism has two effects upon the believer. The first, the seal or character, is indelible, as the fathers had taught. The other effect, God's grace, could be lost. The *sacramentum* was the seal, the *dominicus character*, literally "the mark of the Lord," that the rite conferred. The rite, not the minister, imparted this likeness of Christ to the believer. While this likeness could never be lost, still the individual could lose the other effect—God's grace—by his or her decision to sin.[13]

After the sixth century the theology of sacramental character underwent no development and only reappeared as a topic of theological investigation in the twelfth. In the thirteenth century Thomas Aquinas revived the Augustinian notion of indelible character, based as it was on the biblical metaphor of a seal and the patristic analogy of branding a soldier. Rooted in baptism and evident in confirmation and holy orders, character was for Thomas a matter of a new relationship between God and the individual believer. Distinct from grace (which sanctifies the essence of the soul), character is a modification of one's spiritual (and thus intellectual) power. God has given the sacraments for a twofold purpose, to remedy sins (by grace) and to perfect souls through worship of God. Christians, therefore, have a purpose to which God has deputed them, so that they need to be sealed in that service. A character is a spiritual seal, a spiritual empowerment for the action of glorifying God, the physical evidence of which is observable in the "sensible sacrament," the perceivable rite.[14] Since Christian worship is a participation in Christ's priesthood, sacramental character is the mark likening the Christian to Christ the priest, perfecting the spiritual power natural to every human soul. Since the subject of character is the soul, in its "intellective part, where faith resides,"[15] and since intellect is eternal (perduring beyond bodily death), so is the character conferred in those sacraments that empower believers for divine worship.

Although theologians contemporary to or after Aquinas varied with him in their understanding of certain aspects of sacramental character, his writing on the subject proved most strongly influential on the Roman Catholic Church's official teaching.[16] In the twentieth century the Second Vatican Council produced its Dogmatic Constitution on the Church, describing baptism as incorporation into the church, "the priestly community," and baptismal character as the faithful being "destined" to Christian religious worship.[17] While in continuity with Aquinas's teaching, the council's explanation of sacramental character bears a stronger ecclesiological tone, resonating with its renewed images of the church as the People of God and Body of Christ. Among theologians who contributed significantly to the council's documents were Karl Rahner and Edward Schillebeeckx, each of whom had developed groundbreaking work in recovering the sacraments as experiences (rather than objects) of grace. Schillebeeckx influentially developed a model of sacraments as personal encounters with Christ in the church, with the church being the primary visible manifestation (the sacrament) of Christ now in the world.

Rahner likewise insisted that the sacraments are fundamentally understandable only within the life and context of the church, the historical and social presence of the salvation brought about by God through the person and mission (the "event") of Christ. The grace of Christ achieves its fullest realization in the lives of individuals sanctified through the events of the church's sacraments. Baptism is the symbol of the reality of a person's incorporation into the church, bringing with it all the other effects that follow from it. The term *character*, the traditional description of this "first effect" of baptism, is suitable so long as "arbitrary mystification about this sign" is avoided (a qualification, no doubt, addressing the Reformation's rejection of the concept centuries earlier). The import of attributing the conferral of a character on the baptized, Rahner beautifully concluded, is "the Church of Christ's express and enduring claim to the baptized person, produced by a sacramental and historical event."[18] Seeing no contradiction between his and Aquinas's explanation of character, Rahner's concern was to articulate how a person shares in the priesthood of Christ through membership in the church.

Bernard Cooke understands sacramental character in an utterly corporate and communal sense, with worship entailing not just cultic liturgical action but the entire life of the Christian community. The community of faith can only exist through the sharing of that faith, which is focused in its formal ritual worship. All of Christian living, however, is to be a consecration to God in love for humanity, that is, an act of worship, just as Jesus' life was. The attribution of priesthood to Jesus in the letters of the New Testament and church fathers is a powerful symbol of God's having revealed in Jesus the consecration of one's entire life in loving service to humanity as the worship of God in spirit and truth (John 4:23). The priestly character of the entire community of faith the church shares with each person baptized. Cooke carefully explains that the character is not the individual possession of each believer but rather the way Christ's Spirit incorporates the person in the church: "This is not an individual modification that comes to each person with baptism; it is the Christian community that is priestly/sacramental in its whole being." The experience of the life of faith, of life in Christ, reaches its peak in the sharing of

we are all modified by each baptism
"No Man is an Bland."

Communion is Thus belonging to a bigger bonding beyond any of us

the Eucharist, "the community's very way of existing as the sacrament of Christ."[19]

A communal understanding of the sacramental character marking all who have been baptized points to the Eucharist as the peak experience for believers' knowing they belong to something that is not only far bigger than themselves but that also exceeds their sum total as individuals. The assurance of that membership, attested by the sacramental character, emboldens us to expect to receive and share grace in the celebration at the table of God's word and Christ's body and blood. Such a corporate, communal view of God's gracious action toward humans, Louis-Marie Chauvet argues, is utterly evangelical: "The gospel is communitarian by its very nature. To believe in Christ is to be immediately gathered together by him who is confessed as 'our' common Lord."[20] Recovering the ancient tradition of the church as Christ calling together his body (as opposed to the modern temptation of thinking of the church as individual believers in Jesus who choose to get together) gives priority to a positive, inclusive notion of sacramental grace. An individualistic notion of grace cannot but amount to reflection on liturgy in terms of a personal transaction or the acquisition of some commodity—"what I got out of it." Historically, an individualistic approach to sacramental practice was aligned with a predominantly negative view of grace, that is, sacraments primarily as ritual means for remedying the sinful state of souls, rather than an empowering share in "the possibility of a different history"[21] that the Spirit reveals through word and sacrament.

The communal ecclesial priority of the celebration of the sacraments corrects the negative connotations that an individualistic view of grace entailed for the complementary notion of the sacramental character. Rather than defining the character in contrast to the continual possibility of losing the state of grace, a corporate view of sacramental grace perceives the Holy Spirit forming the members of the liturgical assembly in the image and likeness of God through sharing in the paschal mystery of the Son. Sacramental character bespeaks the assurance of faith, the church's faith in

22

Christ's presence and action in their midst when they gather to pray in his name. "Such an assembly," Chauvet asserts, "is the Christians' *primary mark* or...the 'fundamental sacrament' of the risen Christ."[22] The biblical notion of such gathering that might come most readily to mind is the Lord's promise in Matthew, "For where two or three are gathered in my name, I am there among them" (18:20). Still, the accounts of the supper on the eve of Jesus' death more pointedly steer us to the roots of the church as the assembly of those sharing in the one cup of the new covenant, drinking deeply of the very life symbolized by his blood.

Church: People Assembled to Share in the Divine–Human Covenant

The primordial term for church is *ekklesia*, best translated in English as "assembly," a word drawing on both Greek and Jewish usage. The former entailed the official designation of regular convocations in Athenian democracy, which connotation St. Justin echoed in his second-century *Apologia* at Rome: "And on the day called Sunday an assembly is held in one place of all who live in town or country...."[23] Within Judaism, however, lie the stronger liturgical-theological implications of the earliest believers' adoption of the term, a concept so elemental to their self-identity as not to be later translated in Latin but, rather, merely transliterated as *ecclesia*.[24]

What formed the escaped Hebrew slaves from Egypt into a people, the People of God, was God's calling them together at Mt. Sinai to enter into the covenant. This originating event in the biblical tradition is the *Qahal Yahweh*, the "assembly of Yahweh." Translated in the Septuagint version of the Bible as *ekklesia Kuriou*, the Greek word for "assembly" captured well the sense of God as the one convoking the people and present in their midst (see Exod 19:17–18).[25] In that assembly God gives his word, with the people responding, and then solemnizes the divine bond with them in a communion sacrifice, the "blood of the covenant" (Exod 24:8). As conveyed in the New Testament accounts of the Last Supper, Jesus evoked that primordial Jewish imagery in establishing the new covenant by means of the words he spoke over the cup, with the Markan version (repeated in Matthew) explicitly designating it as his "blood of the covenant" (Mark 14:24; Matt 26:27). Thus does the tradition reveal the Lord as giving his followers, in the familiar genre of the Jewish communion sacrifice, the bodily, ritual means of his life-sharing presence with them in the wake of his death, the originating event of the new covenant.

To grasp the type of ancient Jewish ritual implied here we must put aside the painful, punitive connotations the word *sacrifice* largely bears in contemporary English usage. Biblical Judaism had a number of different practices we gloss under the generic term *sacrifice*, including but hardly limited to expiatory rituals in reparation for sin. The common thread running through them is best grasped in terms of offering, an act of offering that renders a response or return to God, an offering that unites the people with God. The ritual performed by Jesus on the eve of his execution was of a specific type, the communion sacrifice, for which, according to biblical scholar Xavier Léon-Dufour, Exodus 24 gives the description "par excellence."[26] The importance of recognizing the liturgical-theological link between the Last Supper and the "assembly of the Lord" in Exodus, via Jesus' words over the cup, lies in its indication of the covenantal and communal character of the Eucharist. Contemporary scholarly attention to Jesus' words over the cup is not only or even primarily concerned with what in the second millennium became the debated doctrine of the real presence (of Christ in the bread and wine); rather, it keeps the symbols situated in their ritual action, and the ritual, in turn, situated in its purpose of sustaining and repeatedly renewing the mutual, covenantal presence of God with the people.

Prior to the altar ritual with the blood of bulls, the assembly at the base of Mt. Sinai involved God's giving the people the Law, the Torah, as a way of life, God's way of making a life for the

people, eliciting from them their desire and agreement to participate therein. The ritual then seals the covenant-for-life, with the
blood (typical for the Semitic world) representing life itself, and
its sprinkling on altar (symbolizing God) and people, the commitment of God to them and them to God. What makes this
account paradigmatic yet also unique among all communion sacrifices in the Hebrew scriptures is the direct sprinkling of the
people themselves. Neither a customary nor a repeated gesture in
ancient Jewish tradition, the sprinkling of the people with the ani-
mals' blood symbolizes in a most heightened way the divine–
human communion that *all* such rituals effect when an animal is
slaughtered, its blood offered to God, and then its meat included
in a meal renewing the peace and promise shared as people of the
covenant with Yahweh. The annual Passover meal, of course,
became (and remains, albeit minus the slaughtering of lambs at
the Temple in ancient Jerusalem) the most important communion sacrifice or peace offering practiced by the Jewish people.
The symbols and narratives at the Passover table elicit the urgency
of need and the favor of God toward the Jewish people, as well as
God's power and commitment to see them through deadly passages forward into life. In his reinterpretation of the communion
sacrifice, Jesus draws the identity of God and the people together
by his blood, being "both on God's side by reason of his mission
and obedience and on the side of human beings by reason of his
death."[27]

At the Last Supper, "Jesus' symbolic action," concludes N. T.
Wright, both "deliberately evoked the whole exodus tradition and
gave it a new direction" in the manner of a prophet, articulating
both the people's need for deliverance (redemption) and God's
irreversible determination to renew the covenant through the
long-awaited messianic victory.[28] Wright argues that Jesus' words,
"blood of the covenant," evoke not only Exodus 24 but also
Zechariah 9:9–12, announcing the arrival of the king, riding
humbly on a donkey, who will "command peace to the nations"
(v. 10), and the Lord's restoration of the Jewish exiles to their

stronghold "because of the blood of my covenant with you" (v. 11). The symbolic actions and words of Jesus on the cusp of his death reveal his life mission as ushering in the hour of God's deliverance of the people—the "now" or "today" Jesus repeatedly asserted as the *kairos* or inbreaking of God's reign in the healings and forgiveness he effected for Jew and Gentile alike. Herein lies the power of the eschatological message throughout the New Testament: neither some philosophical rumination about time nor the means to predict cataclysmic future events but rather "poetic and mythic language with which people express their hope for God's justice to come in life-transforming ways."[29] Biblical eschatology is a call to action, a call to join in God's project of bringing much needed justice, mercy, and peace among the struggling and marginalized here and now, a voice of hope empowering the voiceless.

The appropriation of the exodus tradition in the Hebrew prophetic literature, argue Andrea Bieler and Luise Schottroff, is not primarily prognostic descriptions but, rather, relational imagery inspiring life practices working against the grain of history, at times even courageously in the face of death. Jesus' interpretive words over the cup, which Luke and Paul render "the new covenant in my blood" (Luke 22:20; 1 Cor 11:25), shared at the table representing the eschatological People of God, draws them into his life-unto-death, making them sharers, participants in the new life his death is about to inaugurate:

> An eschatological interpretation of the "new covenant" returns to the roots of the phrase in the Torah and the prophets. It is God's saving promise to Israel and, beyond Israel, to all the people of God. This promise lives where it is heard, and it means the beginning of a journey into God's just world....Thus Jesus' words at the supper, when repeated in present time, become an eschatological moment: We, the participants, hear the voice of hope *now*. We are invited to be people of God.

> This tradition of a new covenant is bound up with the vision of healed humanity in which all peoples will have their place, no matter how different they are.[30]

The overwhelming consensus among scripture scholars—including Léon-Dufour, Wright, and Schottroff—recognizes a universal vision within the Exodus covenant and, thus, in biblical and post-biblical Judaism itself. When Jesus in the Markan version describes the cup as his blood of the covenant "poured out for many" (Mark 14:24; Matt 26:28), the allusion to the communion sacrifice in Exodus points further to the content of the covenant: God speaks of Israel as "my treasured possession out of all the people," only to add immediately that "all the earth is mine," with Israel serving as the "priestly kingdom" among all nations (Exod 19:5–6). Likewise, when in Luke Jesus says the cup is "poured out for you" (22:20), the twelve apostles he is addressing represent the twelve tribes of Israel, whose messianic hope in a (new) covenant is for the healing not only of theirs but all nations and, indeed, the entire creation.[31] Here the richness of the Hebrew biblical prophets, in whose lineage the New Testament situates Jesus, comes into play.

The openness God showed to all peoples through his covenant with Israel in Exodus (19:5), as well as Israel's priestly role toward all nations (v. 6), later became symbolically concentrated in David, only to reach heightened universalism in the person of the Suffering Servant. Second Isaiah attests how the servant will astonish "many nations" (52:15) and "make many righteous" by "pour[ing] himself out to death," bearing "the sin of many" (53:11–12). Further along, the universal invitation in Third Isaiah bespeaks the "everlasting covenant" grounded in God's "steadfast love for David," calling "nations that you do not know," who will come running (55:3,5). The universal trajectory of the divine covenant with the Israelites at Mt. Sinai thus became more pronounced and elaborated in the prophetic poetry of the Suffering Servant. Jesus' word over the cup, in terms of the

27

covenantal blood "for the many," bears that promise and, according to Christian biblical faith in him as the Messiah, fulfills it. When believers assemble in obedience to his command to do the covenantal meal in his remembrance, they stand in the presence of the Lord and God whose will is the salvation of all humanity. Indeed, they profess themselves participants in the very life and mission of this God for the life of the world.

The wider body of the Hebrew prophetic literature reveals the intimate sharing of life and spirit God seeks to bring about with humanity, pressing further the gift of the Law as a joining of God's will with people's—a mutual sharing in life. The Suffering Servant poetry signals this through a notable shift in the cultic language found in Isaiah 53:12. The allusion to the poured blood symbolic of the covenant is now described as the servant himself being poured out. The Hebrew reference to the servant (in the NRSV, "himself") is literally to his *nephesh* or soul, to his very life, which Leviticus teaches is "in the blood." Indeed, one's blood is "the life of every creature" (Lev 17:11,14).[32] In this linguistic shift Léon-Dufour identifies a personal, existential character taking the place of the literal cult of the sacrificial blood, eliciting what the law of the covenant is all about: "In the beginning, the law, which expresses God's will, takes the form of a code of precepts, though it is not limited to this. In its source the law is basically God himself expressing his desire and love and seeking to establish a communion with his people."[33] Thus do the Suffering Servant poems resonate with God's words through the prophet Jeremiah: "I will put my law within them, and I will write it on their hearts; and I will be their God, and they shall be my people" (31:33). Moreover, while in Jeremiah the divine promise comes as a "new covenant" (31:31), the prophet Ezekiel conveys God's promise to give the people a "new heart...a new spirit" (36:26), which Spirit is none other than God's very own (v. 27), the gift of God's own self. Once placed "within" them, God's Spirit makes the people follow the divine statutes and ordinances. Indeed, the Law and the Spirit of God are one and, once given anew, establish a most intimate

28

divine–human relationship: "No longer will it be up to men and women to accept the precepts and then do the best they can (offerings and sacrifices, acting justly, etc.) to live in communion with God; now God himself will come and produce fruits of holiness within their hearts."[34]

Here, then, is how the Christian tradition came to proclaim the message of a universal salvation in Christ that was and can still be consistent with the faith of Jesus the Galilean Jew and his followers. Faithfully obeying the command that Jesus gave them on the eve of his departing from them in death, wherein he identified the cup of covenant sacrifice with his lifeblood, the first believers who celebrated him as risen Lord found themselves caught up in the life of the prophetically promised Spirit. The pharisaic Jew Paul of Tarsus, self-professed apostle to the Gentiles (see Gal 2:8; Rom 1:5), claimed the prophetic word from Jeremiah and Ezekiel as the reality of those gifted with faith in Christ. In his second letter to the Corinthians Paul describes the believing community as "a letter of Christ, prepared by us, written not with ink but with the Spirit of the living God, not on tablets of stone but on tablets of human hearts" (3:3). This is the same Corinthian community whom Paul earlier had to admonish concerning their eucharistic gatherings, the very occasion for his recounting the tradition that had been passed down to him (1 Cor 11:23), namely, Jesus' words and symbolic gestures over bread and cup, which he interpreted as "the new covenant in my blood" (11:25).

All of this surely is a Christian theological reading of the Jewish biblical material, but such is the Christian tradition at its roots: believers' efforts to understand what had taken possession of them, namely, God's revelation of salvation through the new covenant in Christ Jesus. A redeeming benefit of this recent biblical scholarship for Christian thought and practice has been the growing effort to correct a triumphalism that has too long asserted the church's religious and moral superiority in terms of what supposedly was (and remains) inferior about Judaism.

Rather than promote the status of the church at the cost of a superseded Judaism, the point is to be humbled before the mystery of what the God of Israel has done in Jesus of Nazareth "for the many," that is, for all peoples, through the power of the Spirit.

The upshot, then, of such a biblical investigation into assembly, covenant, blood, and Spirit is God's empowering people to share in a life of holiness—of justice, mercy, trust, generosity—the life, as we saw further previously, that early believers in Jesus as Lord called "spiritual worship" (Rom 12:1). As Christians, then, we must be vigilant to keep our own cultic house in order, so to speak. We must correct any tendencies to see our assembling for Sunday worship as an affirmation of our human—social, religious, political, or national—superiority so as, rather, to participate gratefully in a vision of the good life with God that we could never conceive, let alone sustain, on our own. Indeed, the permanence of this covenant, this life-giving communion, comes from God, whose will cannot change, who by nature is faithful. But that is the very point of retrieving the traditional notion of sacramental character, as we found at the end of the previous section. When construed in a thoroughly ecclesial and biblical sense, the concept asserts the priority and assured promise of God's calling together the assembly as a priestly people, of the church's permanent claim on each of the baptized as members of the Body of that Christ Jesus whose faithfulness to the God of the covenant (Torah) made him the very personification of the life-giving Spirit. The seal of the Spirit is not an individual's possession; rather, the Spirit, the Lord himself (2 Cor 3:17), takes possession of the baptized so that they might be "transformed into the same image" (v. 18), glorifying God through lives animated with the very heart he has placed within them.

Life in the presence of this God is what in modern terms might be called a highly personal reality; indeed, this is how Léon-Dufour, writing a few decades ago, characterized the Christian appropriation of the universal salvation wrought by the "personal sacrifice" of the Suffering Servant.[35] Such a characterization, however, is highly susceptible to individualism and abstraction, to lapsing into spiritualities that can become obsessed with self-realization while failing to discern how much our very selves are shaped through our bodily existence, how our personhood is thoroughly physical, social-cultural, and traditional.[36] No, in order for Christian imagination to take shape we must, in more postmodern fashion, attend to the reality of assembled *bodies*, to "the encounter of real bodies with texts, symbols, concepts, sounds, smells, and the interaction of bodies with each other in ritual activity."[37] To believe and live in relationship with the biblical covenantal God requires relationships as and among the people that God has committed to forming among every race and nation. Herein lies the irreducible Christian need for assembling, the real way to meet our desire to come to know this God so often and easily hidden in the ambiguities of our bodily—physical, natural, social, cultural—lives. The glory of this God resides in faithfully bringing human lives into full, conscious, active participation in the love revealed through the paschal mystery of Christ, lives of worship, of spiritual sacrifice, coming to light in the liturgy.

A "Certain Violence" in Assembling: Liturgy as Interruption

None of us, whether individually or collectively, adequately lives up to being sacraments of the crucified and risen Christ, for our imaginations are an orchestration of so many bodily influences and encounters that, in relation to the Gospel's vision, can range from harmonious to distracting to downright dissonant (sinful). It is the assembling that reveals what God is up to, and assembling precisely for the celebration of word and sacrament, which provide "profound and rich insights into the inner reality, not directly perceptible in itself," of God's working out human salvation in history.[38] We come from the anonymity of our worship of God in and through our daily lives "with all [our] rough edges, slow-wittedness, mediocrity, and limitations,"[39] to the peak

31

or summit of that worship, powerfully conveyed and shared through the liturgy's symbols, not the least of which is the assembly itself. In this undeniably secular age the tacit, if not at times explicit, thoughts in the minds of individuals as they gather together for liturgy may well be something like, "I'm not crazy; I'm not alone in my faith." This, at least in part, is the postmodern challenge for believers. Whereas until a generation or two ago people lived in towns, urban neighborhoods, or rural areas with church congregations functioning as their primary social bodies and, moreover, these as entailing mutual physical presence, today people increasingly practice social contact through electronic media, all the while passing anonymously by scores of others as they execute their personal telecommunications. In the very act of assembling, then, participation in the liturgy replenishes a faith practiced for the salvation of the world, but a world that no longer perceives the church as the heart of the town square or Sunday worship as a norm for good social standing. But is that such a bad thing? Maybe a return to the biblical roots of assembling, such as I have attempted in this chapter, can refresh our sense of call, mission, and identity in the eucharistic liturgy. After all, what most characterizes humanity in the Gospel is people's awareness of their profound need for God. *and each other — if only as a*

With the assembly constituting the fundamental symbol of *check* the risen Christ and, thus, the primary agent of the celebration,[40] *on* the ritual act of gathering is highly significant. Reflecting on the *our* social and interpersonal costs the earliest Christians had to pay *sanity.* for practicing the faith—such as alienation or even outright rejection from their families or misunderstanding and suspicion on the part of workmates and neighbors—Robert Cabié proposes what was unique about their assembling:

> While [members of the early communities] did find brothers and sisters in the assembly, the bond was the joy which faith gives but which also has to bridge human distances in order to accept the gift of a love that is from

Community — an assembly of people who know they need one another.

32

The social cost of discipleship

the Lord. During the time of celebration they had to do
a certain violence to the social order that reigned in
their everyday lives.[41]

Cabié's talk of "a certain violence to the social order" necessitated
by Christian assembling is provocatively instructive, for it highlights the power exercised by ritual in the establishment and
maintenance of a social entity *as* that social entity. This human
power can only *analogously* be called an act of violence, since one
of the hallmarks of ritual is its power to shape the visions, com-
mitments, and beliefs among a society's members precisely by not
having to resort to physical force or intimidation. The "certain
violence" in the early Christians' assembling, Cabié argues, lay in
their crossing class lines, redistributing wealth, and rejecting
familial customs by addressing each other as kin in Christ, taking
up a collection for the needy in conjunction with bringing forth
bread and wine for the Eucharist, and so forth. Indeed, current
historical scholarship is building our appreciation for how the
Sunday dinner assemblies of early Christians were social experiments bending the boundaries of social relations.[42]
　　Turning to our contemporary era, members of the church
find themselves in situations analogous to that of their ancestors.
The evangelical tension that exists between the vision of the kingdom of God revealed in Christian liturgy and the flawed, often
unjust structures and practices that pervade societies and churches
establishes the sort of ritual "violence" that is essential to
Christian worship. The tension will perdure as long as the Lord
calls the church to carry on its mission in a fallen world ever passing before his resurrection and future coming. Still, while the
term *violence* here succeeds in conveying how serious the stakes
are in the church's assembling, the term may be too provocative
for its own good in a late modernity so riddled by the actual
forms of violence visited upon individuals, communities, and
entire peoples. For that reason we might rather think in terms of
disruption, in a manner reminiscent of German political theolo-

gian J. B. Metz's characterization of the Gospel as *interruption* of whatever prevailing social conventions are proving destructive of human subjects.[43] In our time, Metz argues, the Gospel liberates by interrupting the dehumanizing forces within the relentless evolution of scientific technology and market economies, both of which roll over the lives and sufferings of individuals and peoples in the pursuit of anonymous progress and profit.[44]

To Metz's call for the traditional practice of liturgy as an irreducible source for both confronting and consoling Christians in their faith, Don Saliers responds with a careful explanation of how this comes about through the *assembly's eschatological art*:

> *at least this!* Among the requisites for participation in the form, content, and dynamism of Christian worship, two are central: a sense of wonderment and awe at the mystery of God's becoming flesh, and an awareness of suffering and the interdependency of all things....The sense of mystery and awareness of suffering is given specific focus and meaning in the whole sweep of the scriptural witness to God. Furthermore, while a general religious or even philosophical sense of wonderment at being may be brought to the forms of Christian liturgy, the central fact is that the texts, symbols, and ritual actions with ordinary elements of the earth reconfigure our general awareness. And the central broken symbol of Christ, crucified, humiliated, and problematic draws into itself the suffering of the world.[45]

The assembly's work is a highly purposeful act and, as such, a type of revelation, if we attend to how its social and symbolic proclamation of the Gospel, through words, signs, and gestures, disrupts our conventional knowledge of "the way things are." The liturgy can only do this, that is, it can only dispose our thoughts and emotions to the divine mystery given through shared human reality, *as ritual*. As a type of ritualizing, the liturgical assembly requires believers to step aside from the order (or perhaps, discord) of daily life into a bounded time and space that is "performed, embodied, stylized, repetitive, rhythmic, collective, patterned, traditional, deeply felt, condensed, symbolic, dramatic, paradigmatic, transcendent, adaptive, and conscious."[46] As ritual, liturgy reorders our personal, social, and traditional bodies so as to hear and respond to that word of Christ otherwise hidden in the joys and hopes, sorrows and fears within and among the faithful, the community, and wider society.

The notion of "liturgical space" takes into account all of the various material elements of the liturgy and how they function together in the celebration of a given rite.[47] These physical, bodily elements include such stable features as the baptismal font, altar table, ambo (reading table), and presidential chair, each of which by its structure and placement symbolizes the irreducible roles of word, sacrament, and ministry in the life of the church, members of Christ's Body. There are, moreover, numerous elements whose selection varies according to particular rites, seasons, and pastoral occasions: music and chants, objects such as flowers or candles, the use of certain gestures, postures, or movements, as well as the roles of different ministers and the assembly. All of these—people, architectural fixtures, movable objects, sounds, silence, and actions—both relate in their own ways to beliefs in the Christian tradition and relate within a particular liturgy to one another so as to create in that ritual enactment a concrete encounter with God in Christ. Rather than begin here a discussion of these many elements of the liturgical space in relation to the work of the assembly, I address them as they arise in our exploration of ministerial leadership and stewarding of the liturgy in chapter 4, below, "Leadership for Christ's Body."

A Humbling Presence through Participation

The nature of the church's liturgy, founded in the paschal mystery of the crucified and risen one, necessitates its being practiced in ways that mediate the presence of God found in the *midst* of the dynamic ritual interplay of proclaiming and responding, leading and following, seeking and finding, feeding and sending forth. We must not lose sight of the humbling fact that such ritualizing—the doing of liturgy—is the human action of a divinely assembled body of human beings. This liturgical reality is humbling because it confronts us with the revelation of how far and wide and deep the self-emptying love of God in Christ continues to reach through space and time. It is humbling not only because of this faith dimension, however, but also because of the remarkably subtle phenomenon that human symbolizing itself is, a process in which deep, hidden levels of meaning can only become known and shared by risking the activities and engaging the images that comprise the ritual. Hiddenness, therefore, is endemic to the liturgical assembly both in its divine dimension as the presence of Christ and its human dimension as symbolic ritual agent of that presence.

The paschal mystery is celebrated so that the many members of the church, the People of God, might acquire "the same mind...that was in Christ Jesus, who, though he was in the form of God...humbled himself and became obedient to the point of death—even death on a cross" (Phil 2:5–6,8). Given the ambiguity of our human sacramentality, as well as that of the multiple components comprising liturgy's space, the assembly must trust in the Spirit's will and power to shape all together into an encounter with their risen Lord. The discernment of the Spirit in the practice of the church's liturgical traditions requires continuous recourse to the biblical word of God that Spirit has inspired. To that mode of Christ's presence in the liturgy we now turn.

Chapter Two

Holy Scripture
Revelation of the Mystery in Our Time

Worship Infused with the Word

Assembling is the primary symbolic means of Christ's presence in the eucharistic liturgy and, thus, for the church. The words and actions that transpire in this gathering are paradigmatic for all the ways believers live and act as members of the risen Christ's body now in the world.[1] But in order for the assembly to reach its ritual climax of communion in the body and blood (the very person) of Christ, the entire liturgical space—people, ministers, room arrangements, music, and so forth—must be infused with the biblical word of God. The specifically Christian character of the human activity of liturgy comes from the divine revelation afforded by the Spirit through the proclamation of God's word. To assemble at the table of God's word and Eucharist is an act of humility: not the false and humanly destructive humiliation that despotic power visits upon the weakened but, rather, the freeing humility that pervades the stories and psalms of the Bible, wherein people come to recognize themselves and others honestly in the presence of God. The power of that word resides in its ability to shape the imaginations of those who hear and respond to it. Assembling to hear the word requires a genuine submission to the Gospel, real faith trusting in God amid the full range of our human strengths and weaknesses, joys and sorrows, virtues and sins. The assembly enables our encounter with the Christ of the

Gospel and *his* God, as opposed to our and others' fantasies of what perfect existence would be like.

In revealing the Torah as a way of life shaped against the horizon of God's justice, patience, and love, Jesus instructs his followers, "Be perfect, therefore, as your heavenly Father is perfect" (Matt 5:48). It is not hard to imagine how threatening or impossible those words might sound if taken out of context, that is, if imagined through some other lens than that of the entire Gospel. But the question always comes down to whether or not those assembling are ready to hear God's word about what is and was and will be. For those members who are not so disposed, the experience of liturgy falls short. They are left only to their own imaginations, left the poorer for having decided in advance, perhaps too quickly or resolutely or even bitterly, what God's reign is like. For God's is not a reign limited to our personal histories—with all their traces of triumph and tragedy—but, rather, is one that calls us to hear our story as part of one much larger, at times comforting, at others confronting us. A story from my own pastoral past may serve as a vehicle to illustrate what is at stake, what is possible or can possibly be missed, in the invitation to word and sacrament amid the assembly. In the course of my narrative I italicize several technical terms that will shape the liturgical theology of the word of God to follow.

A Tale of Trouble Turned Teachable Moment

Some years ago I was asked by the priest who directed the Roman Catholic campus ministry at the university where I was studying to substitute for the regular liturgical musician at the community's Sunday morning Mass. That weekly liturgy, along with another in the evening, took place in the university chapel, a contemporary structure with excellent acoustics and a fine pipe organ. The Sunday evening Mass was usually attended by some hundred or more undergraduate and graduate students, while the morning liturgy (unthinkably early for most students) assembled a smaller group of graduate students, professors, their spouses and families, as well as some others from the area who had made it their primary faith community. It was a typical American Catholic campus ministry situation, I would argue, in its demographics and numbers, albeit at one of the more prominent research universities in the country: a relatively small yet significant percentage of the total population of Roman Catholics affiliated in some way with an institution of higher education, mostly white and middle class. Typical of such situations, as well, was the fact that the music at the Sunday morning Mass was prepared and led by a volunteer, a man in his thirties playing guitar, with a few other people comprising a rather informal choir (in this case, five early-middle-aged women). In asking me to provide the liturgical music for the one Sunday morning, the priest made clear to me not only his primary need for a substitute but also his awareness of my ability as a classically trained organist. He said that he thought it would be good for the congregation to hear the instrument that otherwise stood silently by the sanctuary when they celebrated each week. I was happy to oblige and prepared the musical settings for the acclamations (Alleluia, Holy, Lamb of God, and so on) that this assembly normally sang each week so that they might not feel too disoriented. As for the opening and communion, I would try for seasonally appropriate hymns that would be familiar to a fair number of American Catholics.

I was needed for a date in late November, in the closing weeks of the *liturgical year* but also just before the American civil-religious holiday of Thanksgiving. We were in *Year C* of the *lectionary cycle*, hearing passages from the latter chapters of the Gospel of Luke. The date for which I was needed turned out to be the thirty-third Sunday in *Ordinary Time*, the penultimate Sunday of the church year, for which the Gospel reading would be an excerpt (vv. 5–19) from Jesus' *eschatological* discourse in chapter 21 (vv. 5–36). That passage, reworking the *apocalyptic* material from its source in Mark 13, maintains bracing images of the end: upheavals that will be cosmic (plagues, famines, earthquakes, celestial signs), societal (wars and insurrections), and ecclesial, visited directly upon believers themselves in the form of persecution (by family members, friends, synagogues, and governments). In the face of all this, Jesus exhorts his followers to a perseverance based on the faithfulness of God's promise of salvation (Luke 21:18–19) and confidence that the Lord himself will give them words when put on trial (Luke 21:15). In conjunction with this eschatological Gospel passage, the first reading for that Sunday is an apocalyptic *pericope* from the book of the prophet Malachi, foretelling the dreadful "Day of the Lord" (a common theme in the Hebrew prophets), when fire will incinerate "all the proud and all the evildoers" while the healing sun of justice will rise over those who fear God's name (Mal 3:19–20).

As I set about preparing that November liturgy, those biblical passages did not surprise me. The liturgical year, with nuances variable to each of the Synoptic Gospels (Matthew, Mark, and Luke) governing the three-year cycle, always ends on a strong eschatological note. My job was to choose ritual music that would serve this closing phase of Ordinary Time. I was delighted to discover that the hymn, "Come, Ye Thankful People, Come," long associated with the American holiday of Thanksgiving, was largely a paraphrase of another eschatological passage, a parable with its ensuing explanation, found at Matthew 13:24–30, 36–43. Jesus tells the story, unique to Matthew's Gospel, of the weeds that the enemy planted among the wheat and the master's instruction not to pull up and burn them until the harvest. To his inner circle of disciples, Jesus gives an apocalyptic explanation of the parable. The wheat are the "children of the kingdom" whom the Son of Man sowed in the field, that is, the world, while "the weeds are the children of the evil one" (37–39). He goes on to describe "the end of the age" as follows:

> The Son of Man will send his angels, and they will collect out of his kingdom all causes of sin and all evildoers, and they will throw them into the furnace of fire,

where there will be weeping and gnashing of teeth. Then the righteous will shine like the sun in the kingdom of their Father. Let anyone with ears listen! (Matt 13:41–43)

Thus, the suitability of the hymn lay in its being not only seasonal to the American holiday but also based on an apocalyptic text utterly resonant with the lectionary at the close of the church year. In addition, the content of the hymn's scriptural text (Matt 13:36–43) has some of the very same images found in the passage from Malachi that would serve as the first reading that Sunday. The full text of the hymn is as follows:

Come, ye thankful people, come,
Raise the song of harvest home:
All is safely gathered in,
Ere the winter storms begin;
God, our Maker, does provide
For our wants to be supplied;
Come to God's own temple, come,
Raise the song of harvest home.

All the world is God's own field,
Fruit unto God's praise to yield;
Wheat and tares together sown,
Unto joy or sorrow grown;
First the blade, and then the ear,
Then the full corn shall appear:
Lord of harvest, grant that we
Wholesome grain and pure may be.

For the Lord our God shall come,
And shall take the harvest home;
From the field shall in that day
All offenses purge away,
Giving angels charge at last

In the fire the tares to cast,
But the fruitful ears to store
In God's garner evermore.

Even so, Lord, quickly come
To your final harvest home;
Gather all your people in,
Free from sorrow, free from sin;
There, forever purified,
In your presence to abide:
Come, with all your angels, come,
Raise the glorious harvest home.[2]

This beautiful text, set as it is to an uplifting tune, could not, it seemed to me, be better suited for the entrance hymn of the Mass that Sunday.

When that Sunday morning arrived, however, things seemed quite different to the small band of choir members who showed up for their customary quick and sole rehearsal prior to the service. I proposed my playing the tune through once and then all singing the entire four verses as a way to "warm up" our minds and voices. Upon reaching the end of the last verse there was a strained silence followed by the choir members telling me, as one voice, that they refused to sing the hymn. I was as taken aback by their reaction as they were by my choice of the hymn. They found it "offensive," as one member bluntly put it, and they would have no part of singing those words. I explained that the bulk of the text was directly drawn from one of Jesus' parables in the Gospels, as well as utterly resonant with the Gospel reading for the Mass that morning. These facts seemed not to matter to them in the least; they were unmoved by my argument from scripture and tradition (that is, the liturgy). Exasperated, I remarked that if they had such a serious problem with this Gospel-based hymn, they had better plan on being offended by Jesus' words in today's *proclamation* from Luke and, moreover, from the first reading in Malachi. None deemed my advice worthy of response. We moved on through the rehearsal without difficulty. When I opened the liturgy with the hymn as planned, the choir stood with mouths closed in protest while the congregation, to varying degrees, joined in the familiar melody and words.

What to make of such an experience? I have taken pains to describe the situation in some detail so as to acknowledge here, however briefly, the possible issue of gender difference in this confrontation, as well as the typical pastoral dynamic of choirs being on edge with substitute directors (unhappiness over the absence of the familiar leader with whom the choir is comfortable—a phenomenon I have experienced repeatedly as a choir member myself). While those factors may detract from my main argument for this chapter, I mention them so as not to do anybody in this real-life scenario an injustice. Be that a helpful digression or not, this memory has remained so strongly with me over the years because I understood this to have been an acute experience of many American Catholics and other "mainstream" Christians' rejection of, or at least lack of openness to, the eschatological and apocalyptic dimensions of both the Gospel and the liturgy. While I failed to share a successful conversation with those few women about why they found the text so offensive, I am quite certain that the problem for them lay in the unequivocal imagery of final judgment, of God's reckoning with the just and unjust, of angels carrying out God's definitive plan, purging and purifying and, in the end, destroying the wicked. This imagery does not sit well with those whose God must be envisioned always as gentle, accepting of all in a nondirective manner, open-ended toward each person's plans and life projects, whatever they may be, not to mention those of society and the wider world. It would seem that professing that "God is love" excludes asserting that God will judge. But that leaves us without any expectation that *God will act*. Such expectation is fundamental to biblical eschatology.

To interpret that hymn, and thus Jesus' eschatological-apocalyptic parable, only in negative terms, focusing exclusively on the purging and burning as (apparently) the work of a cruel God, entails a highly skewed, imbalanced hearing of the text. There may be any number of personal reasons for individuals to receive the message so negatively but, again, such pastoral considerations are beyond the primary scope of this chapter. What begs articulation here is the utterly hopeful character and purpose of the hymn (and thus, the apocalyptic Gospel passage), which apparently is *evident only to those who know they hunger for it, who know their utter yearning for the boundlessly merciful God of Jesus finally to bring about his promised reign of justice and peace for all of creation.* The hymn is an anticipatory celebration of gratitude, of thankfulness for God's keeping us in safety, providing for our needs, delivering us from evil (shouldn't that phrase sound familiar?), freeing us from sorrow and, yes, from *sin*, bringing about, at last, the glory befitting a divine life fully shared among humanity. The hymn is joyful as it moves from proclaiming, in the indicative voice, the character and actions of the God of Jesus to beseeching, in the imperative voice, *this* God to "quickly come" and bring about the "home" he has promised. But is that not also a description of what the church does each time it celebrates its liturgy? To fail to proclaim passionately and intelligently, to hear openly and earnestly, to receive honestly and humbly, and to celebrate longingly and hopefully the apocalyptic-eschatological readings at the end of the liturgical year, as well as those in Advent (the year's beginning), is to reveal a tragic misunderstanding of why the church celebrates the liturgy at all. I say tragic because it leaves people, for all their painful hungers and good desires, tasting only a bland approximation of the real food and real drink (see John 6:55) of Jesus and his word in the liturgy.

As for the misunderstanding, I would propose that much of it lies in the question of what it means to say that through the proclaimed word of scripture Christ *comes* to the people assembled. The nature and experience of this coming hold the keys to understanding Christ's presence in the service of the word and, with that, the entire liturgy. Clearly, the "word of God" is not simply a matter of the pages of the Bible somehow speaking directly and univocally to all. That those assembled hear, that is to say, receive and interpret, biblical texts in different ways is readily evident in the scenario I have just recounted. So what, then, is the "word of the Lord"? The question is fundamental to the belief that God is "living and active" (Heb 4:12) in the midst of the church and world. An exploration into the fundamental theology of the *word of God*—the next step in this chapter—explores God's revelation as an encounter through the word (1), one that the tradition holds most powerfully occurs in the liturgical assembly. This necessitates further consideration of how the liturgy takes its shape biblically through the course of the *church year* and the patterns of scriptural texts in the *lectionary* (2), all of which together foster the church's encounter with the total image of the risen Christ Jesus. The final step examines how this paschal imagination governs the *proclamation* of the diverse of range of biblical texts (3), such that the members of the assembly may respond to and appropriate in their lives the word of Jesus, "Today this scripture has been fulfilled in your hearing" (Luke 4:21).

Christ Comes: The Word of God

The proclamation of the word of God in the liturgy renders explicit the presence of the Christ who is hidden amid the church's assembly and diffused through its members in the world. The contents of the proclaimed words of scripture bear the touchstones for discerning how God is present and active at a given moment and place in human history. Biblical texts are the means whereby the crucified and risen one forms his people in his own image, through the power of his Spirit. "I will not leave you orphaned…," Jesus assures his disciples gathered with him at supper on the eve of his death. "The Holy Spirit, whom the Father will send in my name, will teach you everything, and remind you of all that I have said to you" (John 14:18,26). The first generations of Christians not only experienced the power of that Spirit animating their lives as the church but also came to recognize in letters attributed to Paul and other apostles the working of the Spirit through the word. The process evolved even further as the stories about Jesus told at the Sunday eucharistic assemblies were eventually written down and edited into what became the Gospels. Thus did the Christian church come to expand its scriptures beyond that of the received Jewish texts they regularly proclaimed in their prayerful gatherings. More than that, the ancient Jewish concept of the word of God conveyed in the scriptures took on a further, definitive meaning in the person of Jesus the Christ, whom in the power of the Spirit they proclaimed as the blessed one who comes in the name of the Lord (see Mark 11:9).

The word of God that the church proclaims in its liturgy, then, is something far greater than words on the pages of a book, and this for both human and divine reasons. Humanly, the various types of literature comprising the Christian Bible have the potential to shape imaginations, instill hope or fear, convey knowledge and wisdom, and inform intellects and consciences in the ways that all good stories, poetry, and prose do. Furthermore, the contexts in which texts are encountered affect their impact, such that solitary reading or silent study comprises a different experience from that of public performance or group recitation. Reading or hearing a text is always an event for those involved, for it draws people into an encounter with symbols—words evoking images and ideas—that interact with, create, reinforce, or transform a world of meaning for those engaged. The sharing of words, whether written or oral, comprises the medium for a relationship between persons. Speech and texts are the means for reaching across the distances inherent to our differences to join in the venture of knowing, bonding with, even loving one another, whether that be on the scale of a social-political body or interpersonal friendship.

Biblical faith reveals the encounter between God and people as coming about precisely through the creative, symbolic media of words. Indeed, the Hebrew experience of being in relationship with the Lord God was such that the concept of "word" itself became a primary symbol for how the totally other and unapproachable divinity reaches out to humans, creating and sustaining them:

> In the minds of the biblical authors God's mighty actions and God's word were so closely connected that they had only one word for both—*dabar*. That word carried a sense of energy, of dynamism, like something that pushes or drives one forward. The word of God carried the power of God. It was creative; it brought forth what it promised.[3]

While ancient Judaism had many metaphors expressing God's interaction with people (angel, hand, arm, finger, wisdom, and so on),[4] the prophetic literature capitalized on the notions of the "word of the Lord" and God's spirit (*ruach*, "breath") as particularly apt expressions for God's ineffable difference from all creation and yet his intimate engagement in the lives of creatures, especially the affairs of humans and the course of their histories.

The synchrony of word and the breath (spirit) that propels speech found its convergence in the first believers' articulation of what God had revealed, and thereby done, in the person of Jesus of Nazareth. Drawing on the metaphors of the Hebrew prophets and Wisdom literature, the Gospels reveal him as the word made flesh (incarnate) through the power of the Holy Spirit. Jesus' brief public mission was in the genre of the classical Jewish prophets. Uniquely possessed by the Spirit (as revealed at his baptism in the Jordan), Jesus' words and other symbolic actions were those of God, such that God's will was enacted and their effectiveness assured in their very speaking and doing. Jesus' ultimate self-gift in obedience to God's will and love for humanity came in the seeming disaster of his death and the marvel of his resurrection, the paschal mystery that required his disciples to rethink all they had experienced with him. As of Easter Sunday, the only Jesus his followers knew and could encounter was the risen Lord, the full revelation of whose identity shed light back on all he had said and done. Those words and deeds, henceforth remembered and shared by the gathered community, reveal what God's love and will for humanity (that is, the reign of God) is like. If followers of Jesus desire to know him, that is, to encounter his person and share in his presence, then they must hear anew the accounts of his deeds, his relationships with the crowds and individuals, and the contents of his parables, proverbs, and other sayings. Every Gospel narrative is reflective of the entire scope of the word of God in the Old Testament, the Jewish scriptures; the Gospels express this in terms of Jesus' fulfilling the Law and the prophets (see Matt 5:17; Luke 24:27) or the very word of God coming to dwell with humans, full of grace and truth (see John 1:14). Jesus' self-offering in death and vindication in the Spirit proved his entire life to be the ultimate communion of God with humanity, humanity with God.

As we saw in the previous chapter, on the eve of his death Jesus reached into the Torah for the ritual pattern of God's covenant with the people at Mt. Sinai to create the ritual-symbolic means of his ongoing personal relationship with his followers, his friends (John 15:14–15), as the new covenant in his blood. Just as in the Sinai event, the content of the covenant was made explicit in its proclamation to, and reception by, the people and then sealed in the sacrificial blood and the meal shared (Exod 24:1–11), so the eucharistic assembly is an event of divine word proclaimed, human response given, and covenant bond strengthened in sacrament. The irreducible value and utter necessity of this ritual for the ongoing life of believers as a church lies in the symbolic nature of *divine revelation*, which biblical theologian Sandra Schneiders succinctly defines as "God's accepted self-gift to human beings."[5]

Revelation, the primary referent of the Christian "word of God," only occurs when God's symbolically conveyed gift of self (and thus life in its fullest) is received, felt, appropriated, shared by people—a two-way street, so to speak, of active encounter and commitment. Revelation, in biblical tradition, is a matter of relationship, of mutual presence. Insofar as humans are a party to this relationship, revelation is of necessity a bodily event borne of participation in symbols, and especially language. In the Jewish heritage the experience of God is thereby personal, an invitation to communion with a God intimately engaged in the lives and corporate history of the people. Given the pain of that history, the revelatory relationship with God is also messianic, that is, mindful of God's promises of the past and expectant of God's future deliverance according to God's word. Christians embrace Jesus as that Messiah, the "definitive self-gift of God, the Word of God incarnate,"[6] exceeding all expectations, yet do so precisely through the symbolic medium of bodily activity. Even in the crucified and risen Christ (Messiah, Son of God) the mystery of divine revelation remains a humanly shared reality greater than the symbols and words that convey it. God, in Christ the Word, humbly submits to loving, mutual sharing through such symbolic activity, as it is the only means whereby (bodily) humans can become more fully what God envisions with and for them.

The undeniable ambiguity of symbolic engagement in this world necessitates the ritual tradition of word and sacrament for Christians, the corporately accepted and shared site for interpreting with God and one another the signs of God's reign as living and active in our midst. The word spoken anew, "today" (see Luke 4:21), in the service of the word and written on our bodies through sharing in the sacrament of his body and blood, nourishes us as members of a mystical Body of Christ far greater than the sum of ourselves or even the church as a corporate social entity. We share in the messianic life generated by the vision of that day when, through Christ, God will be all in all (see 1 Cor 15:28).

At any one time the faithful at worship receive and share the exceeding magnitude of that vision, of that revelatory word of God, in pericopes, in passage-units of scripture, in slips cut from the whole tree of life ready to take root in the soil of our lives. Just as we humans can be personally, mutually present only in limited fashion and yet do not doubt (in fact, unreflectively assume) that we are really, fully there with one another, so the biblical revelation of God can be received and shared only in doses that nonetheless bear the whole. Just as certain stories among friends, families, or larger social bodies are both powerful in detail and paradigmatic of their entire relationship or total common bond, so the individual passages of scripture shared in the eucharistic assembly send us "back to the totality of revelation," that is, "the mystery of Christ Jesus."[7] Thus are the table of the word and the table of the Eucharist inseparably one act of worship in the church.

The faithfulness of God to us, the constancy of grace promised in Christ, is revealed (offered, accepted, and shared) in the ritual familiarity and repetition of the words, food, drink, and gestures at the eucharistic table. The nourishment at the table of God's word must provide a full board of texts from the sacred scriptures so that Christ might come and "speak" to us in ways that both meet the breadth of human experience and convey the entire range of literary genres and content in the Bible, especially the four Gospels. While God's love, and thus the substance of revelation, does not change, we humans certainly do in our capacities and openness to receiving and responding to that word. This may be due in some instances to sinfulness, but the larger reason lies in the changed circumstances of our lives, such as those due to one's life cycle, health, personal and social circumstances, and so forth. Passages from certain genres of scripture (such as Wisdom or the prophets) or particular stories (whether from the Old Testament or the New), even though heard before, sound different in a given time or place, eliciting a new response and, thus, an original moment of revelation. Furthermore, in our humanity we are limited as to how much we can digest in one ritual moment, that is, during one liturgy.

The church, then, orders selections of biblical readings for the service of the word over yearly cycles. The church year and lectionary of readings are liturgical traditions that enable Christ genuinely to come to the members of his body so that they might know the presence of his divine, loving mystery working out in the varied courses of their lives through time. The way the church

American Airlines®

oneworld

BOARDING PASS

PASSENGER NAME
BOLLMAN/RICHARD

FROM:
MINNEAPOLIS/SAINT P

TO:
CHICAGO ORD

FREQUENT FLYER #

RECORD LOCATOR
HKHDHR

FLIGHT
AA3753

CLASS
N

DATE
09JUN

DEPARTS
945A

GATE
E14

BOARDING TIME
915A

SEAT
14B

GROUP 3

001703660722

American Airlines®

BOARDING PASS
BOLLMAN/RICHARD

FROM:
MINNEAPOLIS/SAINT P

TO:
CHICAGO ORD

DATE
09JUN

FLIGHT
AA3753

CLASS
N

DEPARTS
945A

SEAT
14B

GROUP 3

RENT WITH AVIS OR BUDGET AND EARN 50
AMERICAN AIRLINES AADVANTAGE® MILES PER D

SAVE
UP TO 25%

Present this pass at Avis, visit
avis.com or call **1-800-331-1212**
to book. Mention **AWD # K817167**.

Terms and Conditions: The savings of up to 25% applies to Avis leisure weekly and weekend rates and is applicable only to the and mileage charges of the rental. Offer does not apply to car group X. Taxes, concession recovery fees, vehicle license recovery customer facility charges ($10/contract in CA) may apply and are extra. Optional products such as LDW ($29.99/day or less, e in Louisiana $49.99/day) and refueling are extra. Please mention **AWD # K817167** to receive this offer. Offer is available for U.S. Canadian residents only for rentals at participating locations in the U.S. Offer may not be used in conjunction with any other number, promotion or offer. Weekly rates require a minimum five-day rental period. Weekend rate available Thursday noon; car be returned by Monday 11:59 p.m. or higher rate will apply. A Saturday night keep and an advance reservation may be requ **Discount valid on rentals checked out no later than December 31, 2012.** Offer is subject to vehicle availability at the time of r and may not be available on some rates at some times, including some online rates at **avis.com**. Car rental return restrictions apply. Offer subject to change without notice. Holiday and other blackout periods may apply. Renter must meet Avis age, drive credit requirements. Minimum age may vary by location. An additional daily surcharge may apply for renters under 25 years old.

Avis features GM vehicles.   ©2011 Avis Rent A Car System, LLC   20

Save up
to 20%!

Show this pass at Budget, visit
budget.com or call **1-800-527-0700**.
Mention **BCD # U072412**.

Terms and Conditions: The savings of up to 20% applies to Budget leisure weekly and weekend rates and is applicable to the time and mileage charges of the rental. Offer does not apply to car group X. Taxes, concession recovery fees, ve license recovery fee, customer facility charges ($10/contract in CA) may apply and are extra. Optional products such as l ($29.99/day or less, except in Louisiana $49.99/day) and refueling are extra. Please mention **BCD # U072412** to receive offer. Offer is available for U.S. and Canadian residents only for rentals at participating locations in the U.S. Offer may n used in conjunction with any other BCD number, promotion or offer. Weekly rates require a minimum five-day rental pe Weekend rate available Thursday noon; car must be returned by Monday 11:59 p.m. or higher rate will apply. A Saturday keep and an advance reservation may be required. **Discount valid on rentals checked out no later than December 31, 20** Offer is subject to vehicle availability at the time of rental and may not be available on some rates at some times, including so online rates at **budget.com**. Car rental return restrictions may apply. Offer subject to change without notice. Holiday and c blackout periods may apply. Renter must meet Budget age, driver and credit requirements. Minimum age may vary by local An additional daily surcharge may apply for renters under 25 years old.

Budget features Ford and Lincoln vehicles.
©2011 Budget Rent A Car System, Inc. A global system of corporate and licensee-owned locations.   20

American Airlines reserves the right to change the AAdvantage® program and its terms and conditions at any time with notice, and to end the AAdvantage® program with six months notice. Any such changes may affect your ability to use the awa or mileage credits that you have accumulated. Unless specified, AAdvantage® miles earned through this promotion/offer do count towards elite status qualification. American Airlines is not responsible for products or services offered by other particip companies. For complete details about the AAdvantage® program, visit **www.aa.com/aadvantage**. AmericanAirlines AAdvantage are marks of American Airlines, Inc.

keeps time from one Sunday to the next, year after year, is intimately connected to our need to hear and respond to the whole range of God's word offered to humans.

Hearing and Responding to the Word over Time

The distinct way in which the earliest generations of Christians reckoned time was simply from Sunday to Sunday. Believers in Jesus as Christ (Messiah) and Son of God lived in expectation of the new age of God's reign breaking into this world, a new heaven and a new earth. Although the cataclysmic imagery of ancient Christian apocalyptic texts has led many contemporary readers, across the ideological spectrum, to assume that the earliest believers comprised a world-renouncing religion that expected an immediate obliteration of the planet Earth, such a simplistic view has not held up under the best of historical, biblical scholarship.[8] Revelatory of the overturning of the world as they knew it, apocalyptic narratives were the imaginative, and thus empowering, symbolic language through which Christians maintained hope amid poverty, social alienation, and/or political oppression in their day.

Even decades ago, Orthodox theologian Alexander Schmemann argued brilliantly from the perspective of earliest liturgical practices that the first generations of Christians did not reject time and this world for some sort of otherworldly religion. That, after all, could only amount to the heretical separation of the God of creation from the God of redemption. The evidence that those first believers did not fix an exclusive gaze on the Lord's second coming lies in the multiple attestations, Christian and otherwise, to the early churches' keeping of the "first-eighth day" as the "day of the Eucharist," as an "established day" for the eucharistic celebration: "The eschatology of the new Christian cult does not mean the renunciation of time. There would have been no need for a fixed day (*statu die*) in a 'wholly world-renouncing' cult, it could be celebrated on any day and at any hour."[9] Recently, German Prot-

51

estant theologians Andrea Bieler and Luise Schottroff have articulated the import that this practical eschatological imagination had for the New Testament communities. The ancient eucharistic gatherings proclaimed the inbreaking of God's reign as a reality at hand for the living. Sharing in the body and blood of Christ made tangible the otherworldly love, fellowship, and justice of the coming Son of Man that could be practiced in everyday life: "The Eucharist celebrates the nearness of God and allows us to experience with our senses the taste of the real life God wills."[10]

Linking the celebration of the Eucharist, the paramount liturgical action of the church, with the specific day of the week, Sunday, is of critical importance for the renewal of the church, which is to say, *of the Christian life,* today. It is not simply the liturgy in itself that constitutes the source and summit of the church's power and activity[11] but, rather, the liturgy as celebrated on the Day of the Resurrection, the Day of the Lord. The unprecedented, new belief that God had raised the crucified Jesus from the dead emboldened the early believers to take up and transpose the biblical, prophetic symbol of the Day of the Lord, as well as the Jewish apocalyptic notion of the Eighth Day as the first day of the New Creation, and apply them to what God had done in Christ.[12] Herein lies the heart of Christian eschatology, namely, that the biblically inspired faith in the establishment by God of a new era, the time of God's reign, has indeed definitively happened, *but* in a way we humans would not expect. The power of God's reign, which is for the salvation of creation in history, flows from the wounded hands and side of the risen Christ, establishing the mission-activity of believers as their carrying on in their bodies and bringing about with their hands the mercy and forgiveness, justice and peace of God's reign on earth, witnessing to God's favor (grace) to all in Christ until he comes in glory. Sunday is, as Vatican II teaches, "the original feast day,"[13] the day for gathering to celebrate the ritual of word and sacrament whereby in the power of the Spirit we gather up the work and witness of our lives throughout the week in a sacrifice of praise and thanksgiving, so that the Lord might give us the nourishment at the table of the word and of the Eucharist that alone can sustain us on the journey toward the kingdom's final coming.[14]

The liturgy is able to carry out its evangelical mission for the church and the world only if it continuously articulates anew the paschal mystery in the times and places of our lives. This means that the attitude with which believers are to approach it is ultimately not fascination at the wonder of God's coming to us in the confines of symbolic elements but, rather, an uncomprehending yet consoling submission to the revelation of the *kenotic* (self-emptying) pattern of salvation in Christ that at once satisfies our hunger for God and sets us off again with yearning desire to encounter this singular love in the myriad circumstances of our time. Louis-Marie Chauvet makes the point brilliantly: "Rather than '*How* can God (it being understood that *we know who God is*) do such and such?' would it not be more in keeping with biblical revelation and especially with the 'scandal of the cross' to ask '*Of what God* are we speaking when we say that we have seen God in Jesus?'"[15] Scripture alone provides for believers the images and narratives—in such various genres as history, mythology, prophecy, psalmody, Wisdom, apocalyptic, Gospels, and apostolic letters—that at times console and at others confront us with the God of Jesus. Otherwise we are left to slip, whether comfortably or despairingly, into some other god-images of our own making.

In order to renew the liturgy's power to nourish the encounter with Christ they envisioned, the fathers of the Second Vatican Council perceived that the proclamation of scripture needed both to recover an integral role in every rite and, in the case of Sunday Eucharist, to cover a far greater range of biblical texts through a cycle of years.[16] This would be a matter of seriously revising the lectionary, the ordered series of selected passages (called pericopes) from the Bible to be read (the Latin noun is *lectio*) on consecutive Sundays through the year. Lectionaries of one sort or another have existed since the origins of the church, most likely inspired by the tables of biblical readings for services in Jewish synagogues, some of which seemed to have a three-year cycle. To the "Law and the prophets" Christianity added the continual reading of the Gospels and epistles (eventually comprising the New Testament canon, or official collection of books). While monasteries (East and West), with their complex daily, weekly, and annual cycles of prayer, developed lectionaries primarily on the principle of continuous reading of Old and New Testament books, by the middle of the second millennium the lectionary for the Latin missal had just a one-year cycle of selected passages from the epistles and Gospels. This meager place for scripture in the liturgical life of the church (the lectionaries for daily Mass, as well as for seasons and feasts were likewise poor) is what Vatican II mandated be reformed.

In 1969, just four years after the council, the efforts of biblical and liturgical scholars resulted in the new *Lectionary for Mass*, a development that Presbyterian theologian Horace Allen observes "was to have a profound effect on the worship of the entire Western church, far beyond any expectations of the Roman authorities."[17] In the English-speaking world Protestant communions inspired by the new Roman lectionary formed the ecumenical Consultation on Common Texts, which in 1983 published the Common Lectionary, an adapted version of the Roman table of readings that, after further refinement, is now known as the Revised Common Lectionary (1992). Thus today, Sunday assemblies in Roman Catholic, Anglican, Episcopal, Presbyterian, Methodist, Lutheran, and other Protestant communions all engage a three-year (A, B, C) cycle of scripture readings, anchored by continuous readings of one Synoptic Gospel in each year (Matthew, Mark, and Luke). Pericopes from John occupy most of each Easter Season, as well as some weeks of Lent in Year A and several weeks in Ordinary Time in Year B (which needs filling, as Mark is a relatively short Gospel). The service of the word also includes continuous readings from the epistles, as well as a first reading from the Old Testament followed by a thematically related psalm. With the exception of the Lent-Easter cycle, the Roman Catholic lectionary selects the first reading in relation to the content of the given

Sunday's Gospel pericope. This principle of selection echoes the ancient Christian reading of the Hebrew scriptures as foreshadowings (*typoi* or "types," in Greek) of the person, actions, words, and events of Christ. Various Protestant bodies, however, found this typological selection pattern unacceptable, and so the Revised Common Lectionary has two options from the close of the Easter Season through the end of the liturgical year: semi-continuous reading through the major genres of the Old Testament literature or, alternatively, typological selections related to the Gospel reading.[18]

Acknowledging the variations in lectionaries throughout history as well as the current differences between the Roman Catholic and Protestant lectionaries' approaches to the first reading, David Power nonetheless gets at the liturgical principle fundamental to ordering the biblical readings in the context of celebrating the Eucharist:

> Whatever the immediate purpose and practice in the choice of scriptural texts for services of worship, the hope and intent are to hear the Gospel of Christ, the Word of the Lord given to us in him. As one pair of authors deftly state, "authentic gospel…is talk of Christ which is (1) faithful to the remembered Jesus and (2) free response to the futurity of the risen Jesus." Even if the typological readings of earlier times, present also in the selection of liturgical readings, seem too far today from the original meaning of the scriptures, we share with this approach the purpose of hearing what is proclaimed through the prism of faith in Christ.[19]

That prism is the paschal mystery, the death and resurrection of Christ. This is why the church needs the Sunday Eucharist, the original Christian feast, the prism placed on the table of the word through which are refracted our lives as participation in the mystery of Christ.

Still, the metaphor needs to be stretched further, for the mystery itself has many facets. The length and variety of the canonical

Gospels show this. In each, the passion and resurrection narratives constitute the climax of the revelation of God in Christ Jesus, and yet many chapters that narrate the words and actions of Jesus lead to that climax, shedding further light on the paschal mystery through the details of his word and deeds in the company of people. The prism metaphor for the paschal mystery, one could say, stretches further into a multifaceted gem, numerous surfaces related yet angling off one another: individual bodily sickness and health from birth through death, social and political harmony or strife, participation in religious tradition as recurring invitation to trust in God, power struggles with civil and religious authorities, the quest for freedom in society, the pain of prejudice and the struggle to overcome ancient ethnic divisions, the consolation of love and mutual support of family members, and so forth. All of these human joys and sorrows animate the Gospels, leaving us with no doubt that the risen Lord of creation and history is not alien to any person's or people's lives, in whatever situation the passage of seasons may find them.

Just as the prism of the paschal narratives (of Jesus' passion, death, and resurrection) expanded into so many facets of the human condition as expressed in the four Gospels and the entire canon of scriptures, so the primordial feast of Sunday inevitably broadened into a yearly cycle. The evolution of the church year began with the annual celebration of Easter in the second century, which expanded into a fifty-day season concluding with Pentecost, a "week of weeks," as one fourth-century bishop put it, drawing the faithful into reflection on Christ's resurrection, bodily ascension, commissioning of the apostolic church, sending of the Spirit. In that season the story of Christ becomes the story of the church, as a body, as his mystical Body. The governing role of Easter in the development of the church year continued with the designation of its preceding fast days, only eventually to expand into a forty-day Lenten period of penitential preparation for the great feast. The entire Easter cycle, then, came to span some ninety days, pivoting on the alignment of Easter Sunday with Passover, the Jewish festival during which Jesus was executed.

In those early centuries there emerged also a Christmas-Epiphany cycle around the Roman calendar's winter solstice. With significant variations in theological emphases among the ancient churches ringing the Mediterranean, this cycle was and remains focused on the manifestation ("epiphany," in Greek) of the divine Word in the person of Jesus, with the gradual development of a season that prepares to celebrate his coming (advent). Today in the West the Christmas cycle is comprised of an Advent Season that begins four Sundays prior to the Feast of the Nativity (December 25), and then a Christmas Season following through January 6, the Feast of Epiphany, which commemorates Christ's manifestation to the nations in the persons of the magi who visited the infant child (see Matt 2:1–12).

After Epiphany come weeks for ordered reading through the Synoptic Gospel assigned to a given year (A = Matthew, B = Mark, C = Luke), beginning with the account of Jesus' baptism in the Jordan, the manifestation inaugurating his public mission. In the Roman Catholic church year these weeks between the seasons of Christmas and Lent, as well as the long period following Easter's conclusion on Pentecost Sunday until the end of the year in late November, are called "Ordinary Time," by which is indicated a continual, ordered reading through that year's Synoptic Gospel, along with an ordered plan of other scriptural readings. Other churches, however, have the custom of counting those weeks as "After Epiphany" and "After Pentecost," respectively.

Thus, while Sunday is the primordial Christian feast, the wisdom of the organic development of the liturgical year, beginning with the annual celebration of Easter in the second century and expanding from there,[20] becomes evident. Easter constitutes the center of the liturgical year as it heightens our celebration of what we profess to participate in each Sunday, namely, our belief that God has fulfilled the new covenant in Jesus' blood, in his life given unto death, that is, in his paschal mystery. That mystery's story, however, is not yet finished, even for Jesus: "He will come again in glory to judge the living and the dead, and his kingdom will have no end." This creedal faith that we profess during the renewal of our baptismal promises each Easter, as well as each Sunday toward the end of the service of the word, is our response in faith to the Christ who has once again come to share his life in that proclaimed word. The ordered readings throughout the year, as the introduction to the *Lectionary for Mass* in the Roman Rite articulates, "are aimed at giving Christ's faithful an ever-deepening perception of the faith they profess and of the history of salvation."[21] This is history, however, not as the *study* of past events, as if history only concerned ossified matter whose outcomes are concluded. On the contrary, the history of salvation is as much a matter of what God, through the Spirit of Christ, is working out with people and has yet to complete.

In the Liturgy of the Word (and, in a different manner, the Liturgy of the Eucharist to which it leads) we remember the covenant promises God has made so as to live with an at times reflective, at others expectant, and still other times urgent hope in God's bringing those promises to fulfillment.

> The many riches contained in the one word of God are admirably brought out…as the unfolding mystery of Christ is recalled during the course of the liturgical year, as the Church's sacraments and sacramentals are celebrated, or as the faithful respond individually to the Holy Spirit working in them. For then the liturgical celebration, founded primarily on the word of God and sustained by it, becomes a new event and enriches the word itself with new meaning and power.[22]

The creative, life-giving power of the divine word lies in its Spirit-inspired yet humanly conveyed capacities to shape the imagination of those who proclaim, listen, and respond to its multifaceted content. Like all engagement with written texts, the liturgical celebration of the word of God entails interpretation, a truly complex

58

human affair that when executed within a community requires some guiding principles. The prism through which the Christian community as liturgical assembly interprets the wide range of biblical texts in its lectionary cycles is *paschal*. The dynamics of this paschal imagination govern the liturgical celebration of the word and shape the encounter of the assembled with the living Christ.

Appropriating Christ's Word: The Power of Paschal Imagination

There is "the one word of God," and yet in the Christian Bible that word comes through dozens of texts of various genres spanning several centuries among them and now two millennia and more reaching us today. This means that the human enterprise of interpreting texts is inevitable as the assembled community of faith proclaims and responds to the lectionary readings in a given celebration of the Eucharist. But there is a distinctive, indeed unique (because divinely inspired) interpretive key by which the faith of the community celebrates the Liturgy of the Word, namely, belief in Jesus the Christ as the very Word of God incarnate, risen, and now present in the power of the Spirit active in the church. We profess him as the fullness of revelation. The story of the mysterious risen Lord's Easter Day journey with the disciples on the road to Emmaus (Luke 24:13–35) is the biblical paradigm for how Christ comes through the proclamation of the word in the liturgy: "Then beginning with Moses and all the prophets, he interpreted to them the things about himself in all the scriptures" (Luke 24:27). The disciples were despondently making their way out of Jerusalem, the disastrous site of Jesus' execution, back to the familiar shelter of home, as would only be natural. They were befuddled because Jesus' shameful, accursed death negated their expectations for him, their expectations of what the Messiah would be like, what he would say, do, and ultimately achieve among and for the people of Israel. And so they were left to pick up the pieces in the world as they knew it. The resurrected Christ comes, however, to grace them with an interpretation of his life and death. Through that paschal interpretation he changes their messianic assumptions and, with those, their way of hearing and appropriating "all the scriptures." The event of that word, its transformation of them in the present moment of that Sunday, opens up an original appropriation of the biblical words from the past. Claimed as their own through their hearing and responding to the risen Lord—"Stay with us" (Luke 24:29)—the biblical words from the past lay claim on them, opening into a future into which they can once again move enlightened, nourished, joyful.

The Easter story of those disciples on the road with the Jesus, moving full circuit between Jerusalem and home, moving from proclaimed word to blessed bread, broken and shared at table, is the content and pattern for Christian liturgical celebration every Sunday. Still, no assembly of disciples, that is, of the baptized, could possibly sustain in one service of the word the Lord's interpreting for them the Law and prophets and, indeed, all the scriptures. Hence the need for a Sunday lectionary that cycles through three years, thereby allowing us to hear the full range of the four Gospels as well as continuous, semi-continuous, or selected readings from both testaments of the Bible. The first act of interpretation comes in that very ordering itself, in the priority given to the four Gospels in relation to the seasons and, in turn, the selection and alignment of the other biblical readings—all so that Christ might again come in a new event of revelation in the lives of the assembled and, through them, for the life of the world.

While the generative, mythical story of the road to Emmaus depicts a complete and perfect delivery of Christ's word through an interpretation of "all the scriptures," the church's effort at crafting and executing an ordered movement through the whole scope of the scriptures is never without points for debate, challenges to address, and perhaps flaws to correct. There have been, as I mentioned earlier, any number of lectionaries in various church communities over the centuries, which indicates differences in principles of reading and theology. Recall that the current ecumenical efforts to align the Revised Common Lectionary with the Roman Catholic have realized great measures of success. Yet, a fundamental difference in principle for ordering the first reading has resulted in the churches hearing different passages from the Old Testament from week to week, with the Protestant opting for continuous readings through blocks of the Old Testament literature but the Catholic selecting a passage from anywhere in the canon judged complementary to the given Sunday's Gospel reading. Some Roman Catholic theologians themselves express dissatisfaction with the latter's nearly complete omission of certain genres, such as Wisdom literature, but especially decry the fragmenting and extracting of the texts out of their proper contexts as obscuring "the proper value of the Old Testament."[23] Still, we might recall that Christian churches have varied in their theological methods of reading the Old Testament since the early centuries, with typological reference to Christ dominating in the East (that is, Syria) and allegorical more in the West (that is, North Africa). The challenge today comes in the form of historical consciousness and the extent to which current scientific biblical critical methods should guide lectionary patterns.

Despite the problems with current lectionary construction, Mary Catherine Hilkert observes, "most critics…argue for its revision rather than the rejection of any sort of lectionary…because the lectionary broadens, rather than restricts, the scope of preaching."[24] The lectionary delivers preacher and people alike from the temptation to chain the word of God (see 2 Tim 2:9), to limit how much they are willing to hear, to have challenge and surprise and shape them, to appropriate into their lives. Here we may recall the story from my pastoral-liturgical experience of many years ago, my tale of the choir who took complete offense at the apocalyptic readings from both the Gospel and Hebrew prophetic literature, refusing to hear those words as of God or to begin the possibility of appropriating them at least through the singing of that hymn. Beyond the strangeness of biblical apocalyptic there are today other problems inherent in the cultural-historical worlds behind various scriptural passages, such as sexism, patriarchy, anti-Judaism, racism. While some ministers and communities practice outright avoidance of offensive texts, others take them as a pastoral occasion for critical wrestling that, if pursued always from the perspective of discerning and announcing the Good News of salvation, may well open into a new event of revelation in the assembled community. Moreover, the books of scripture are not mere ciphers of their cultures; they possess and offer a world all their own. Beyond those often difficult social-cultural differences and even at times moral offenses in particular texts lie the unique, original images and messages within biblical narratives, poetry, prophecies, and proverbs, especially the Gospels themselves, which bear such radical words of consolation and confrontation for people of all times and places.

Avoidance of the challenging otherness in scripture amounts to self-imposed starvation at the table of the word. The alternative, as David N. Power compellingly argues, is openness to the infinite God who comes in myriad different word-events:

> To hear the Word as it is given to us, with all its variety of meanings, requires open minds and open hearts.... To listen to the scriptures in their liturgical setting and in their life setting, with the knowledge of what they have meant to tradition, is to listen with the readiness to be challenged. In effect, this is proper to the very nature of human existence, where the power of a word is incalculable. [25]

The challenge and promise for the Liturgy of the Word, then, lies not only in the theological question of how to select and order the biblical readings through yearly cycles but also in the socio-cultural context of their proclamation, that is, the disposition of those to whom the word comes. For, to return to the Emmaus story, just as the two disciples were talking among themselves before the mysterious Christ joined them on the road, so also the members of a given liturgical community bring to the assembly worldviews shaped by culture, social class, traditions, gender, as well as personal and shared histories and current events. In a globalizing and multicultural church, this means that the proclaimed word in liturgy may sound not only new but even intrusive due to the otherness of not only the biblical world of the past but also the diversity, interaction, and at times collision of cultures in the pluralistic world of the present.

> This too is the Word of the Lord and asks for response. The more a person or a community allows this kind of word to affect their way of seeing things, the more one is opened to a horizon of reality that seems without limit. In very truth, the more we open mind and heart to stories that come from others, the more we may be aware of a call to hear a word from beyond, a word that precedes all beginnings to which we can give circumstance or date. All these strange words that we hear speak to us of a voice behind all voices, an address that cannot be precisely located or dated....Such attunement to an address from the infinite and a call to the infinite capacity to hear and to respond is a necessary disposition of the soul in listening to the scriptures as God's Word.[26]

Thus is the proclamation of the word in the assembled community an event of openness of humans to God and one another, a complex and even at times ambiguous or conflicted event, at that. The question of discerning divine revelation within the word-event remains, which, in the liturgical assembly, cannot be other than in terms of the paschal mystery of Christ.

To grasp how the Word of God is living and active in individual biblical pericopes as well as the entire celebration of a Liturgy of the Word, theologians have taken recourse to modern philosophies of hermeneutics (textual interpretation), especially those of Hans Georg Gadamer and Paul Ricoeur. The key principle for our purposes here is the recognition that every text bears a surplus of meaning. The possibilities of meaning inherent in a given composition of words is not limited to the intentions of its author but, rather, emerge in each reading of the text itself, drawing upon the intentions, biases, limits, and original insights the given readers (or hearers) of the text bring and generate in their engagement with it. Hermeneutics attends to the world behind a text, that is, to its historical and cultural conditioning, as well as to the conditions of the present context of those who engage it, that is, the world "in front" of the text.

Bringing the perspective of Christian faith to the hermeneutical process, and recalling how the word of God is not simply identical to any book or even the canon of scriptures, Hilkert explains that the texts of the Bible bear a history of both sin and redemption. "Some of that sin is recognized and named as such within the text itself. Other aspects of sin (e.g., slavery, ethnic exclusion, anti-Semitism) have been recognized and named by the church only from a later cultural perspective."[27] Services of the word must be both *sacramental*, disclosing divine presence in particular times, people, and places, as well as *prophetic*, challenging and confronting individuals, structures, and even liturgical practices that limit or block disclosure of the paschal mystery.

Revelation, then, proves an ongoing history of salvation, with the content of the scriptures being "critically appropriated from the perspective of the new creation into which Christians have been baptized,"[28] especially in the liturgy, where the Spirit works to realize in them "the freedom of the glory of the children of God" (Rom 8:21). This is the "paschal imagination" the Spirit shapes in the members of Christ's Body, anchoring them to the foundational Christ-event of the past while empowering them to weigh every proclamation of the word, embedded in biased cultural frameworks, against the vision "of the final liberating reign of God"[29] revealed through Jesus' death and resurrection. The paschal imagination is the work of Christ's Spirit who, even when the preaching misses the mark or subverts the message of the texts, can work through the liturgy's play of different readings, psalmody, symbolism, and biblically infused prayers to inspire participants yet to hear and respond to the word of God. That imagination takes shape in their bodies, as together assembly and ministers move to the table of the Eucharist, where the word becomes most real: "O taste and see that the LORD is good" (Ps 34:8).

Chapter Three
_____

Eucharistic Communion
Christ's Abiding Presence

Sharing from the One Table: Word and Eucharist

If paschal imagination is the key to the service of the word, this is because the purpose of the entire liturgy is to make us participants in the paschal mystery, sharers in the very life of God bestowed in Christ. The whole trajectory of the liturgy pivots on the proclaimed word of God. The introductory rites, with their hymnody and prayers themselves inspired with biblical content, prepare the assembly to hear and respond to the texts of scripture as Christ comes alive through the power of the Spirit in the context of this time, this place, this people. The response, however, is not just a matter of ideas or principles (mere words, one could say) generated by the people but, rather, their further acceptance of the invitation to the table of the Eucharist, where the Spirit makes communion in the life-giving Word a bodily reality. The assembled faithful move from the proclamation of the biblical word to the eucharistic prayer, "the Church's central proclamation of how what happened once for all is actualized here and now in an ever new experience of grace through the paschal mystery."[1]

Here, St. Augustine teaches, the mystery of the intimate union of our lives with Christ's, of ourselves as members of his body now in the world, is proclaimed so as to elicit our life-committing response:

Thus, if you wish to understand the body of Christ, listen to the Apostle, who says to the believers: You are the body of Christ and His members (1 Cor 12, 27). And thus, if you are the body of Christ and His members, it is your mystery that has been placed on the altar of the Lord; you receive your own mystery. You answer "Amen" to what you are, and in answering, you accept it. For you hear, "The body of Christ" and you answer "Amen." Be a member of Christ's body, so that your Amen may be true.[2]

This mutual abiding of Christ in us—members of his Body as church, branches on him, the vine (John 15:5)—is what the Spirit initiates at baptism and nourishes at the one table of the word and Eucharist.[3] This is what is meant by the sacramentality of our Christian lives and, thus, why the liturgical sacraments are needed as revealers of that abiding presence of the Word of God, of Christ, in the stories of our lives. Participation in the liturgy empowers us to interpret our human story as individuals and corporately, according to the meaning disclosed in the life, death, and resurrection of Jesus. Through the tangible bonds of communion with Christ at the eucharistic table—both in the sacrament of his very body and blood and the sacramental solidarity as members of his Body—we are nourished for the journey, the mission we take up as the privilege of sharing in God's practical love for the world.

The living out of the paschal mystery in our lives is impossible if we bypass the altar table (too often the Protestant mistake), that is, if we think we can hear the word and then go directly into the world to "make it happen." On the other hand, if we bypass the table of the word so as directly to adore Christ in the host on the altar (long the Catholic mistake), we are left to our own imaginations as to who he is and to what sort of life he is concretely inviting us.[4] In either case, rather than "a life-giving spirit" (1 Cor 15:45) working in and through us, Christ functions as an external exemplar of the moral life to be imitated. But even that seems impossible, since popular theology long ago devolved into a certain simplistic narrative of the Son of God suffering and dying on behalf of sinful human sons and daughters: How could anyone even approximate the moral character of the perfect man Jesus (who, when one gets down to it, really is not considered human the way we are anyway)? And how could anyone imagine or perhaps even desire drawing close to such a God, the Father, who sends his darling Son to be born miraculously among humans only to have him cut down brutally in the prime of life in divine retribution for humanity's disobedience? The sadomasochistic drama plays out on a stage over and above the terrain of us "regular" humans. The transaction between the Father and the Son is a matter settled between them on our behalf. The Father sacrifices his Son brutally, at the hands of men; the Son atones for humanity's dishonoring of God. All we can do is shudder at the horrific torture and execution, resolve to do better with our own lives as some small way of "making it up" to Jesus for what he suffered, and hope to be found worthy of the promised heaven the crucified Christ opened for us. The Christian life is reduced to personal resolve and initiative for which divine judgment and reward ultimately wait, rather than a mysterious participation in the life of the Son that God is offering here and now in the power of the Spirit.

The latter wisdom, not of humans but of God, comes only through scripture. "Both the mystery of the word and the mystery of the eucharist send one back to the mystery of Christ Jesus."[5] Thus did the Vatican Council's assertion of scripture as "of the greatest importance in the celebration of the liturgy," with the "restoration, progress, and adaptation of the sacred liturgy" depending on the "warm and living love for scripture," ring of evangelical truth and promise the ecumenical way forward.[6] This chapter's theological exploration of Christ's abiding presence in the sacramental bread and wine shared in the Eucharist, then, looks repeatedly to scripture. First, I explore Christianity's struggle to align the notion of sacrifice, particularly as related to the Eucharist, with the biblical deposit of the faith. The fruits of current theological work on that question point to the revelation of the triune God's self-giving love in the incarnate (fully human) Son as the key to the sacrificial, and thus sacramental, dimension of the Eucharist. The second step, then, is a close look at how the Gospel of John grounds the sacraments in the abiding presence of the absent, ascended Jesus, through the promised Spirit sent by the Father. While John discloses the meaning of the Eucharist in the testamentary form of Jesus' farewell discourse at the supper, other early Christian literature provides cultic resources for the Eucharist as the ritual means for our sharing in that abiding presence of God in the crucified, exalted Jesus. A survey of the eucharistic ritual pattern of taking, blessing, breaking, and sharing—all as an act of remembrance—rounds out the chapter as an appreciation for the Jewish and early Christian roots of the church's real-symbolic communion in Christ's body and blood.

What Sacrifice to Offer?

The impotence of the conventional Christian myth of sacrifice and atonement at the dawn of the new millennium is evident in the "mainstream" churches' struggles for effective influence upon society—locally, nationally, or now globally—and in the lives of individuals. In their efforts to assess how the Christian message has lost its way both within churches and in relation to contemporary people, theologians have turned directly to the symbols that so powerfully dominate Christian imagination: sacrifice for Catholics and atonement for Protestants.[7] While both terms have roots in earliest Christian biblical and patristic literature, where they functioned as just two among numerous symbolic expressions for what God has done in Christ,[8] they became in the second millennium the dominant if not exclusive Christian myth, tragically untethered to the full mystery of the Gospel. By the end of the Middle Ages, sacrifice or atonement theology was reduced more or less to the following: "(1) God's honour is damaged by sin; (2) God demanded a bloody victim to pay for this sin; (3) God is assuaged by the victim; (4) the death of Jesus the victim functioned as payoff that purchased salvation for us."[9]

The crisis that eventually developed in the Reformation was theologically concerned with how humans connect to that payoff, to that salvation. The medieval outcome functioned in the sacrifice of the Mass: Christ the victim (the host, *hostia* in Latin) offered in a non-bloody manner that reprised the slaughter on Calvary as an atoning act of measurable merits that in each execution of the ritual could be applied as redemption for individual souls (of the dead). The reformers raged in their rejection of this concept, asserting that Christ died once for all sinners, whose justification lies only in their personal acceptance of that grace by faith. While differing in theological details and practical outcomes, Reformation leaders inevitably rejected the ritual and theology of the medieval Mass, replacing it with services of the Lord's Supper celebrated as memorials of Christ's death and/or sacrifices of praise and thanksgiving. The Council of Trent reacted in turn, condemning all who rejected eucharistic doctrine as including the real substantial presence of Christ, sacrifice for the propitiation of sins, and the fruits of communion, both sacramental and spiritual (by desire).

Trent's decrees on those various elements, however, were formulated separately and thus lacked integration. The legacy right into the twentieth century was a Roman Catholic theology and practice of the holy sacrifice of the Mass that amounted roughly to an enacted allegory of Christ's execution, for which the climactic moment was (and for so many Catholics, remains) the medieval gesture of the priest elevating his large communion wafer (the host, *hostia*) as the moment when the victim Christ once again really is present. All, priest and people, shared in the moment of the "gaze that saves," with the fruits of the consecration applying to an intended deceased soul as well as variably to those attending, who in general rarely "received communion."[10] In reaction to the isolation of the priestly action of the ordained minister at the altar, and this, moreover, to benefit the dead,

Protestant theology and practice came to focus on the fellowship shared by all at the table of the Lord's Supper. The power of the ritual rested not in the sacred hands and words of the priest but rather in the community's obedient response to the Lord's words of biblical command, "Do this in memory of me." Rather swiftly, however, the communal dimension tended to devolve into a fellowship of two: me and Jesus.

One can safely say that the biblically, historically, ecumenically grounded renewal in eucharistic theology of the past several decades amounts to an integration of the notions of presence, sacrifice, memorial, and communion that tridentine theology left fragmented. That fragmentation contributed to the internal distortions and largely fruitless polemics of Catholic and Protestant theology, rigidly pitting word against sacrament, presence against memory, meal against sacrifice, altar against table, thanksgiving against propitiation. As things turn out, careful exegetical and historical attention to scripture and tradition finds the Gospel subverting all the conventional wisdom of those hardened positions. Set in the key of the paschal mystery, and the trinitarian God of love revealed therein, the seemingly opposed terms fall into their own harmony, albeit sung to the strange (but therefore freeing) tune of the Good News.

The dissonance between the Gospel and conventional and other religious understandings of sacrifice has led some at times to question whether the pastoral and theological effort should not be directed at expunging the notion of sacrifice from Christian liturgy and preaching entirely. Conventional notions of sacrifice entail painful loss and self-denial in the pursuit of some desired benefit, some greater good. Applying the concept to life and worship inevitably casts Christianity in a negative light, a mirthless (and for modern psychology) unhealthy pattern of self-deprivation or codependent denigration. A generic religious view of sacrifice imagines ritual repeated either occasionally or regularly to sustain contact and favor with some divinity. Depending on the nature of the god(s) in question, this may entail expressing gratitude or propitiation or purification through offering the best (unblemished) from crops or herds or (in the case of human sacrifice) the people themselves (beautiful, innocent youth) to express adoration or to elicit reconciliation with perfect divinity. Nothing could be at greater odds with the whole point of the Letter to the Hebrews, the New Testament's most fully developed treatment of sacrifice as a *metaphor* (in the Jewish literary form of midrash) expressing the mystery of what God has done, how God has redeemed us sinful humans, in Christ Jesus.

In the Letter to the Hebrews the imagery of the Jewish priestly sacrifice of an animal's blood becomes the interpretive *metaphor*[11] for Jesus offering his life as a single, perpetual gesture sealing the new and eternal covenant, the perfect worship of God through the sanctification of humanity (see 9:11–14). We need make no further sacrifices in the sense of atoning for our sins, for in his historical humanity Christ, the eternal Son of God, has done this once for all. Hebrews, rather, teaches believers of their participation in Christ's "new and living way," exhorting them to live with assured hope in that heavenly vision, "provok[ing] one another to love and good deeds, not neglecting to meet together, as is the habit of some, but encouraging one another..." (10:20,24–25). To this day, however, the rhetoric of sacrifice tends to defeat this sense of liturgically celebrated faith fostering solidarity and service by casting the work of Christ too much in terms of painful propitiatory ritual, rather than expressing the divine–human union God effects in Christ.[12] It would seem, then, that the concept of sacrifice has too much going against it to contribute positively to the theology and practice of the Eucharist as a sharing in the presence of the risen Christ abiding in the church and, through the Spirit, active in its members.

In pursuing more adequate expressions of the mystery of faith, however, most contemporary theologians recognize the impossibility of eliminating sacrificial discourse from Christianity, not only due to its pervasive persistence but also, some argue, because the complex symbolism of the word *sacrifice* actually does serve well the Gospel's truth. In a lucid article synthesizing Protestant, Catholic, and Orthodox contributions, pastoral theologian Scott O'Brien frames the meaning of sacrifice as it "pertains metaphorically to the life and death of Christ as celebrated in the liturgy." The sacrificial metaphor, not despite but because of its contentious history within Christianity and in relation to world religions, is helpful for getting at what Christian liturgy as celebration of the paschal mystery is all about, namely, "a more fulsome appreciation of God's just mercy and our dignity as partakers of the divine life."[13] Sacrifice, as a general religious phenomenon, is certainly about humans seeking union with the deity but, as ever for Christianity, a more fundamental question must govern the approach, namely, "What god exactly are people talking about?"

A biblically inspired way of framing sacrifice points not to a vengeful or jealous or despotic divinity but rather one whose chief characteristics are justice and mercy and whose chief posture toward humans is to draw them right into heavenly friendship, divine communion. The power of God lies in a communion of persons (Father, Son, and Spirit) who share an intimate love that overflows into creation. When extended to a humanity in the throes of injustice and suffering, the hallmark of that love is "a terrible yet tender mercy"[14] given in Jesus' life unto death. The "costly love of friendship"[15] is the shape divine love takes in humanity. And so love, even from the side of God, knows a necessary pain in surrender if life-giving union is to be born and to thrive freely with and among people. In the new covenant, "sacrifice" denotes both the divine–human relationship's need for ritual sustenance and the inevitable suffering the practice of love for and among mortal, sinful humans entails. The whole affair is shot through with paradox, and that paradox, of course, is climactically located at the cross. The eucharistic liturgy functions as Christian sacrifice by providing both the ritual (in the lineage of the Jewish sacrificial covenant meal) that connects humans to the divine love offered in Christ and the effective, transformative symbol of the unthinkable cost of that love.

God's Glory in Jesus: Mutual Presence in a Fierce, Abiding Love

To think biblically of the Eucharist as sacrifice, keeping word and sacrament together at one table, would normally bring to mind the Synoptic Gospels (Matthew, Mark, and Luke), with their drawing on the Sinai covenant, just as we saw in chapter 1. However, to meditate even more deeply on the mystery of the reality present in the sacramental celebration we do better to turn to John, whose treatment of Jesus' passion and death keeps the paradox of salvation at a provocative pitch by proclaiming this human disaster the defining moment of God's glory. In John's Gospel the mission of Jesus, the meaning and purpose of his words and actions, are entirely oriented to his "hour" (see 2:4; 12:27; 13:1; 17:1), which, as biblical scholar Barbara Reid points out, John develops through a metaphor significantly different from sacrifice or atonement: giving birth to new life.

> There is a unique detail in the crucifixion scene in the Fourth Gospel that brings this theme [of birthing new life] to a climax. After Jesus has died a soldier thrusts a lance through Jesus' side, to assure that he is dead. Blood and water come forth (19:34), the same two liquids that accompany the birthing process. The language of birthing is prominent throughout the whole gospel, culminating with this image of Jesus' death as a birth to new life. The theme is first sounded in the prologue which speaks about those who believe as being born of God (1:12–13). Then, when dialoguing with Nicodemus, Jesus talks about the necessity of being born again/from above (3:3). At the Feast of Dedication (7:38) he speaks about "rivers of living water" that flow from his own and the believer's heart (koilia, which is literally, "womb"), foreshadowing John 19:34. At his final meal with his disciples, Jesus likens the pain of his passion to

74

the labor pangs of a woman giving birth (16:21–22).
All these texts point forward to John 19:34, where the
birth to new life that was begun with Jesus' earthly mission comes to completion in his death.[16]

Note that in John's account of the supper Jesus uses a metaphor
for pain (childbirth), indicating the suffering entailed in his
death. Thus, the self-surrendering, pain-enduring dimension
associated conventionally with sacrifice is not absent in Jesus'
final words during the meal. The key, however, is the end for
which such selfless endurance of pain is freely undertaken. In the
Johannine metaphor it is to give life: But what life? The very life
of God made possible for believers through their mutual abiding
in Jesus, the Son (see 15:4). To elucidate so great a mystery, Jesus,
in John's Gospel, needs five chapters of discourse, making it quite
a different presentation of the Last Supper from that found in the
Synoptic Gospels. As is true for all encounters with difference or
otherness, however, John's unique rendition brings a whole level
of awareness and, thus, revelation of the truth, that otherwise
might be lost on us.

The Last Supper account in John contrasts with those in
Matthew, Mark, and Luke due not only to its extensive length—
several chapters as opposed to a couple dozen or fewer verses—
but also to the complete absence of Jesus' words and gestures over
bread and wine at the table (traditionally called the "institution
narrative"). What modern scripture scholars have made of such a
glaring omission in this Gospel has proven a function of their
biases concerning the meaning and even appropriateness of sacramental rites in the life of the church. Opinions have ranged from
seeing the Fourth Gospel as purposely and polemically antisacra-
mental to concertedly emphasizing and promoting the sacraments. The German Lutheran scholars Rudolph Bultmann
(1884–1976) and Oscar Cullmann (1902–99) were the early
champions of the respective extremes. Here a brief review of the
century-long debate can both inform our approach to John's

account of the Last Supper and also enrich our appreciation of the relationship between word and sacrament in Christ's eucharistic presence.

Bultmann not only pointed to the absence of an institution narrative but also, asserting the evangelist's emphasis on salvation as personal, unmediated union with Jesus, claimed that the three passages clearly referring to the sacraments—3:5, 6:51–58, and 19:34–35—were later additions by an ecclesiastical editor. Writing in a similar vein a generation later, J. D. G. Dunn, a scholar in the Anglo-Protestant tradition, claimed that John combated his community's slipping into "institutional, hierarchical and sacral Christianity" whereby "worship in Spirit and truth was submerged beneath a growing mass of ritual and ceremony."[17] In contrast to Dunn, who perceived in sacramental worship a potential danger to the authentic vitality of the primitive church, the German Catholic priest Rudolf Schnackenburg (†2002) argued that the texts point to a flourishing liturgical life at the very center of the community's experience of Christ's presence. A person experiences salvation through a belief in Christ that, far from being a merely individualistic decision, is a most profound union with the person of Jesus, the revealer of the Father.[18] The unity of Father and Son, which Jesus expounds in his discourse at the Last Supper (see John 15—17), is the source of unity in the church and essential to its mission of leading others to Christ. The salvific union with God in Christ was made present to John's community through the sacraments, which, with their origin in Jesus' death (19:34), function as "testimonies and vehicles of the continuing redemptive act of Jesus Christ (cf. 1 Jn 5:6f)," representing effectively the event of salvation to the assembled believers.[19]

The American Catholic priest-scholar Raymond Brown (†1998) approached the question of the sacraments' function in the saving union of Christ and the believer in a still broader fashion. For Brown the key to properly recognizing the sacramental symbolism in John is the evangelist's "general insight that the life-giving power of Jesus was effective through the material symbols employed in the deeds and discourse of the public ministry."[20] The sacraments per se are only a present reality for John's community, as they live in the time after Jesus' ascent to the Father. To represent the sacraments explicitly in the literary genre of a Gospel would be anachronistic. Nor should scholars read their contemporary concern for precise accounts and theologies (including institution narratives for baptism and Eucharist) into the thought of early Christians. Indeed, the imprecise outlook on the sacraments in John fits that Gospel's pattern of having the deeper meaning of things only understood later.

It is in this sense of a "deeper secondary meaning intelligible to the Christian after the Resurrection" that Brown finds a real, and not merely "peripheral," sacramental interest in the Gospel of John.[21] John's readers are able to grasp the further sacramental aspect when Jesus employs apposite symbolism (most notably water and spirit in 3:5 and bread from heaven/his flesh and blood as true food and drink in 6:51–58), whereas the people in the story with Jesus could only be expected to hear the primary meaning. British Methodist C. K. Barrett likewise insists on the futility of seeking any explicit or developed reference to the sacraments in John, arguing that one must look not to hierarchical or Hellenistic-mystery influences but within the Gospel itself to explain John's sense of the church's sacramentalism. While the people in John's stories grapple with the symbolism in Jesus' teaching, only those imbued with the gift of faith in the glorified Son hear in those words the meaning of the sacraments as their personal knowledge of and "ontological" relation with God (that is, on the intimate level of their very being).[22] Barrett thereby concludes that there is "no sacrament without the word, no benefit in the sacrament without faith, and nothing at all apart from the descent and ascent of the Son of man."[23]

Turning to John's account of the Last Supper, we find Jesus disclosing the ontological meaning of his passion as the glory of the faithful Son returning to the loving Father, who will give their abiding Spirit to Jesus' friends as a share in such great love unto death. Dominating John's account is not the symbolism of the supper table but, rather, this *night* (see 13:30) as the turning point of Jesus' entire mission, the final *hour* disclosing who the Son and therefore *God* is: a communion of abiding love offered for humans to share in mutual, humbling, but thereby life-giving service. This divine–human sharing, however, becomes possible for us only by Jesus' passing through the night, the time when the "world" does what it does only too well, which is, tragically, its worst. Enduring the sort of injustice, inhuman violence, and satanic judgment (altogether, *sin*) so widely inflicted on and among humanity—especially the powerless and poor, and too often in the name of God—is Jesus' way to the Father, his ascent. Divine glory paradoxically unfolds in the very situation people (in Jesus' day, whether Jew or Gentile) would consider most utterly godless, death by crucifixion. It is this meaning of such magnitude that John has Jesus convey in the literary form of a final (farewell) testament, rather than, as in the Synoptic Gospels, recounting the cultic tradition of Jesus' words and actions over the bread and cup.

Both the cultic and the testamentary traditions, the French Jesuit Xavier Léon-Dufour argues, are indispensible for the church. The former provides the symbolic means for the ascended Christ Jesus to remain present to his followers. This is what St. Augustine and theologians thereafter called the *sacramentum*, that is, the symbolic rite itself. In John, on the other hand, the testamentary tradition discloses the *res sacramenti*, that is, the life or ultimate goal signified by the rite. "The 'sacrament' has value only because of the 'thing' [*res*], that is, that which it signifies, namely, Jesus Christ and the love in the Church...since the ultimate purpose of the Eucharist is to intensify in this world that fraternal love which is divine in its origin."[24]

Indeed, John seems to take for granted that once he opens the passage by mentioning Passover, "hour," and "the end" (13:1–2) his readers know that the setting is the Last Supper (with the taking, blessing, and sharing of bread and cup that entailed). Verse 3 has the mere dependent clause, "And during supper," before describing at length Jesus' interior thoughts in rising from the table to wash his disciples' feet. That prophetic symbolic gesture discloses the attitude with which the disciples are to share in this special meal at table with Jesus, an attitude not of superior, lorded privilege but of ready, mutual self-giving love. And so Jesus concludes the gesture by giving the new commandment: "Just as I have loved you, you also should love one another" (13:34). This is how people know—in mind, body, and spirit—their communion with Jesus, know their discipleship, know themselves now as the Lord's "friends" (15:14) at table, the ones graced with the privilege of carrying on his last will and testament.

Jesus' farewell discourse in John is a stellar example of testament, a literary genre that occurs some forty times in the Bible and Jewish apocryphal literature. The basic testamentary form entails a man near death calling together his immediate relatives, the leaders, or even the entire people, characteristically calling them "my children," as does Jesus in John 13:33. The testator bids them farewell in a lengthy exhortation reviewing God's faithfulness to them with him, presenting his life as exemplary of how they now must carry on, especially in communal peace and harmony: "I am giving you these commands so that you may love one another" (15:17). Further testamentary features prominent in John 14—17 include prophetic prediction—"If they persecuted me, they will persecute you; if they kept my word, they will keep yours also" (15:20); the designation of a successor—"the Advocate, the Holy Spirit, whom the Father will send in my name" (14:25); and prayers of intercession to God on the heirs' behalf—"Holy Father, protect them in your name that you have given me....Protect them from the evil one" (17:11,15). In addition, the final gathering of his "children" with Jesus is a meal, a relatively frequent motif of the testamentary genre:

> From the viewpoint of the testator the meal, when it occurs, does not simply serve as a framework for his farewells; it *is* this farewell in action; sometimes it has a cultic context. From the viewpoint of the heirs, the meal

is a sign of communication with the testator (who com-
municates God's favor) and among the heirs themselves
(because of their communion with the testator).[25]

Unique to Jesus' testamentary meal is the nature of such communion, namely, an abiding share in the very life of God as a
mutual indwelling of powerful love in practice, the total abandon
of Father in Son and, through the Spirit, of these divine persons
in Jesus' beloved friends. In this resides the glory of God (see
17:22), pointing to the very heart of the paschal mystery as John
conveys it.

Jesus gives his farewell testament at the onset of "his hour…to
depart from this world and go to the Father" (13:1). The glory of
which he speaks in his departing meal is of a piece with his crucifixion, which paradoxically is exaltation, not humiliation. The cross
begins Jesus' ascent to the Father and, with that, his saving Lordship,
manifesting his power to give eternal life to all who believe, to all
who see "the only true God" (17:3) in this Jesus who finishes the
loving work the Father sent him to do (see 17:4). The community,
in turn, glorifies God (Father and Son) by living in the Spirit that
Jesus gives over (19:30) at his death, with the water and blood flow-
ing from his pierced side signifying baptism and Eucharist as the
life-giving sacraments whereby the Spirit comes to abide in his
friends.[26] The Spirit, the water, and blood all "testify" (1 John 5:7) to
the Christ Jesus from whose flesh they flow, making them the source
of the "presence of the absent one."[27]

Accustomed as we contemporary Christians are to associating the sacrament primarily with bread and body, we might puz-
zle over how in John blood signals Eucharist. But this circles us
back to the sixth chapter's discourse on the bread of life, "a key for
the interpretation of the fourth gospel as a whole, since it has to
do with the mystery of the Lord's presence."[28] As with the farewell
dinner, the timing of this discourse is also just before Passover
(see 6:4), with Jesus using the same terminology of life-giving
presence as in his testamentary meal: "Those who eat my flesh

and drink my blood have eternal life....[They] abide in me, and I in them" (6:56). And so the mystical, symbolic movement back and forth in John (in contrast to the straightforward institution narratives we moderns would prefer) is at play, with all moving toward Jesus' death (on Passover) as exaltation. The mystery of his exaltation as including, rather than following, his death likewise plays out between the farewell dinner discourse, the crucifixion scene, and the resurrection appearances. Most notable for our purposes is Jesus' promise of abiding presence through the Holy Spirit in the supper testament, delivering the Spirit (along with the sacraments) on the cross, and then his breathing the Holy Spirit into them on Easter Sunday night (see 20:22). The latter explicitly sets in motion the time of the church, life in the present era that nonetheless finds its source and meaning in the concrete life of Jesus of Nazareth. The ascended Jesus is experienced as alive and active through the Spirit who abides in the community, in those who have been born of water and Spirit (3:5) and who abide in him through sharing in "true food" and "true drink" (6:55), the effective symbols of his life-giving body and blood.[29]

This mystery as *our* reality is what the church celebrates, shares, experiences, knows every Sunday, every Lord's Day, the primordial Christian feast effectively conveying the life-giving power of the crucified and risen Jesus to his friends through word and sacrament. But the Christian community, as we saw in chapter 2, dwells more deeply on this mystery through the annual Easter Season, the fifty days spanning from Easter to Pentecost. The church does this not so as to reenact Jesus' death, resurrection, and gift of the Spirit as so many separate dramatic events but rather, following Johannine theology, as one continuous ascent glorifying God through the sanctification of his friends "in truth" (17:19).[30] Jesus testifies to the Father in his farewell discourse, "Your word is truth" (17:16); it is that word that unfolds the content of the paschal mystery. Through the Easter Season the church's lectionary cycle, in all three years, has as its Gospel reading on the Second Sunday John's account of Jesus' Easter evening appearance and breathing of the Holy Spirit on the disciples (20:19–31). Later, on the Fifth through Seventh Sundays of Easter, the Gospel is taken from Jesus' Last Supper discourse, a total of nine pericopes (over the three-year cycle) selected from John 13 through 17. The assembled faithful on those Sundays do not find themselves asking why they are hearing *about* the Last Supper when it is already Eastertime (as if the liturgical year were a chronological reenactment of the Jesus story). On the contrary, the successive Sundays of Easter are the time for being immersed in Jesus' Passover-ascent to God as *our* mystery, as our abiding in the Spirit who enables us to remain in Jesus, to bear fruit to God's glory, to love as friends in the one who is the way, the truth, and the life. Such reflection on the meaning of the Eucharist during the Easter Season follows in the church's ancient tradition of *mystagogy*,[31] preaching directed to the recently initiated (while beneficial to all) on the sacred mysteries revealed in the sacrament as our communion, a "share" (John 13:8), in the ascended Lord. Hearing selections from the Last Discourse each year in Eastertide gives us the opportunity to appreciate ever more deeply what we do ritually in every Eucharist we celebrate, week in and week out throughout the year.

Sacramental Rite:
Christ's Presence in Remembrance

The testamentary tradition in John's Gospel treats the Last Supper in the genre of a farewell meal wherein Jesus' parting words to his disciples disclose the profound meaning of the meal in relation to his death-exaltation. John's account reveals the ultimate purpose (later in Latin, the *res*, the "thing") of the symbolism at the table to be a real participation in the love of God that is a self-giving love for and among humans. That participation, however, like all group sharing and communication, can take place only through the bodily activity of symbols, of words and gestures, and these in a stylized, liturgical fashion whose repetition connects generations of followers to the Lord's promised presence in the command, "Do this in memory of me." With those words (see 1 Cor 11:24; Luke 22:19), along with Jesus' proclamation over the bread and cup (in Mark 14:22–25; Matt 26:26–29; Luke 22:17–20; 1 Cor 11:24–25), we may feel as if we are on more familiar eucharistic ground. Indeed, Jesus' words concerning the bread and cup, which accompany his actions of taking, blessing, breaking (the bread), and sharing, comprise the shape and content of the earliest believers' liturgical (cultic, sacramental) tradition. The power in the cultic dimension of the Eucharist resides in the words and gestures, the entire ritual complex, to actualize an encounter with the crucified and risen Lord, whose identity is conveyed through the words of prayer and whose presence is affected by his promised, abiding Spirit.

Since the Reformation period in the West, however, and all the more in the modern spread of biblical fundamentalism around the globe, many Christians have questioned and even rejected what to them seems an excessively complex rite in the Roman Catholic, Orthodox, and Anglo-Catholic traditions. The problem focuses on the lengthy eucharistic prayer (called the "anaphora" in the Eastern churches) that the presiding minister proclaims over the bread and wine. While the content of this form of prayer is suffused with biblical referents, including in most cases the chanting of the "Holy, holy" based on Isaiah 6:3, it is nonetheless not a word-for-word proclamation from the Bible. The exception would be what widely is called the "institution narrative," which midway into the prayer changes its genre from an address to God (extolling God's work in creation and history) to a rehearsal of the Last Supper account of Jesus' words and actions with the bread and wine. The latter amounts to what many Protestants came to consider permissible, namely, a short table service for which the words are a direct reading from a Gospel account of Jesus' words and gestures at the supper as the "biblical warrant" for the cultic action. The long eucharistic prayers and symbolic gestures in the "liturgical churches," they argue, abet the clericalism, magical superstition, and idolatry that cripple the proper vocations of the baptized, diverting them from genuine faith in the biblical God of Jesus. There is historical evidence to support some of that criticism. In fact, the whole impetus and success of the modern Liturgical Movement,[32] with the reform and renewal of the rites in Roman Catholicism and other "mainstream" Protestant churches, resides in the historical, biblical, and theological work of scholars being applied practically in the revised liturgical books and rites. The effort has been to retrieve and follow sound, ancient tradition in ways that enable the active participation of believers in contemporary contexts. Those reforms over the past several decades have nonetheless met resistance and even backlash from the other end of the spectrum, namely, ritual conservatives among Catholics (both Roman and Anglo) infuriated by the loss of obscure language and arcane symbolic gestures that they experienced as mystical, transcendent ritual singularly appropriate to the realm of the sacred.

The nub of the eucharistic liturgical reform comes down to question of how the early church actually obeyed the Lord's command, "Do this." The command refers to the entire liturgical action.[33] Tantalizing and pastorally beneficial scholarly work has included the investigation of how the basic biblical sketch of Jesus taking, blessing, breaking, and sharing came by the fourth century to entail quite complex prayers and rituals all across the Christian churches. It is, indeed, only as late as the fourth century that we have complete, reliably dated texts of extensive eucharistic prayers, homilies, and catechetical instructions on the liturgy and sacraments. One dominant misguided approach to this challenge has been the (anthropologically predictable) desire to find a pure line of practice tracing back to Jesus' words and actions or, put another way, a universal form of eucharistic practice in the early church to which all the current rites should conform. Things are not that simple.[34] Taking, blessing, breaking, and sharing do constitute the basic elements of the cultic tradition, as found in not only the New Testament but also the extremely early (Syrian, perhaps Palestinian) church order, the *Didache*, and the mid-second-century *Apologia* of Justin, martyred in Rome. Still, the exact content and order of those elements of eucharistic celebrations varied from the start, as would only be expected of oral, house-based, local traditions.

The blessing component of the ritual is what I would argue is most important yet hopelessly lost on the biblical fundamentalists in their rejection of robust eucharistic liturgy. The New Testament accounts all mention the blessing as part of what Jesus does *prior* to his words of command, "Take this...eat...drink.... Do this in memory of me." Jesus was a Jew celebrating that meal in the company of his disciples—fellow Jews. We do have solid historical knowledge of what *blessed* would have meant in such a meal context. The historical evidence supports the Jewish forms of blessing as crucial sources in the development of the liturgical eucharistic traditions—in ritual words, symbols, and gestures.

Whether the Last Supper was a Passover Seder (as in the Synoptic Gospels) or a festive meal celebrated a day before Passover (the scenario in John), the basic type of ritual entailed would have been the same, namely, the communion sacrifice or peace offering.[35] Such meals entailed multiple blessing prayers, including one with bread and up to several over cups of wine. Liturgical historians caution us that the earliest textual evidence for Jewish blessing prayers at table is found in the second-century CE rabbinic collection called the Mishnah.[36] That book, along with the Hebrew Bible and literature from the period between the Old and New Testaments, nonetheless provides the bases for outlining what the prayer pattern would have been at the Last Supper and helps explain the shape eucharistic rituals took in the earliest Christian generations. The Mishnah instructs that a *berakah* (a blessing of God) was to be said before anything was consumed, and it provides short *berakoth* (plural for *berakah*) to be said for specific items. If three or more were gathered at table, then one was to say the blessing on behalf of all. While it is doubtful that formally set wordings of blessings for wine and food existed prior to the second century CE, blessings nonetheless were surely said. In addition, while the Mishnah does not provide textual content, it does indicate a well-established pattern of three *berakot* at meal's end, the basic substance of which can safely be assumed to correspond to what eventually became the formal closing grace, the *Birkat ha-mazon*.

The purpose of *berakah* is to praise God for God's favor (*hesed*, "grace") toward the people, with the most basic expression including a dependent clause describing what God had graciously done (specifically or in general). A *berakah*, nonetheless, could be more complex. The *anamnesis* (remembrance) could expand to a full narrative of God's works as the basis for asking God to continue to be so gracious, with the supplication leading back to praise in the form of a closing doxology (praise of God). Similar in pattern—remembrance, supplication, doxology—was another type of praise to God, the *hodayah*, a thanksgiving in the form of acknowledging how God has been gracious that later was rendered *homologeo* or *eucharisteo* in Greek. The tripartite combination of those forms of praise, as found in the later *Birkat ha-mazon*, is found in the second-century BCE *Book of Jubilees*, wherein Abraham delivers a grace comprised of "a blessing of God for creation and the gift of food; thanksgiving for the long life granted to Abraham; and a supplication for God's mercy and peace."[37] Thus, while we have no detailed textual content of the Jewish blessing prayers at meals in Jesus' lifetime, we have ample indication of the pattern that the blessings with food and cups took, including an extended grace at meal's end. For the early church, then, to "do this" in memory of Jesus was to enact a form of communion sacrifice, taking gifts of food and drink in blessing of God, sharing them in fellowship as the people graced by God's faithfulness, and anticipating God's continued favor and deliverance of Israel.

Given the flexibility of wording and content of Jewish blessing prayers in that period, we can understand how Jesus at table could not only highlight or integrate certain aspects of the Jewish remembrance heritage but also even do something utterly new within it. The person who presided over the grace chose the material to be remembered, that is, what gracious deeds and beneficial actions those at table were calling to mind in blessing, which would of course be specific to festival days. The festive framework for the Last Supper is Passover (whether the Seder proper, as in the Synoptic Gospels, or the evening before, as in John).[38] We could well expect, then, that the blessings at the beginning of, during, and at the end of a meal included narrative remembrance (anamnesis) of the exodus, with supplications that God continue to remember Jerusalem, the deliverance of Israel, and the promised messiah (as is prayed at the end of Passover meals to this very day). What Jesus uniquely did was to see "the meal as the appropriate way of drawing the symbolism of Passover, and all that it meant in terms of hope as well as of history, on to himself and his approaching fate."[39]

In Paul's and Luke's accounts of the Last Supper, after Jesus blesses and shares the bread and cup, he expresses his command—"Do this in remembrance [*eis anamnesin*] of me" (1 Cor 11:24; Luke 22:19)—in parallel fashion to YHWH's command in Exodus: "This day shall be a day of remembrance [*lezik karôn*] for you. You shall celebrate it..." (12:14).[40] Scholarly analyses of the Septuagint (the Greek version of the Jewish Bible), the Mishnah, and other sources point to the Greek word for remembrance (anamnesis) in New Testament texts being rooted in the Hebrew term *zikkaron*, a ritual act of commemoration.[41] The words that command remembrance included the entire cultic action that came before, where further similarities in ritual exist between the two texts. In each, the meal takes place on the eve of the crucial divine act of deliverance (the exodus, Jesus' death), with the symbols shared in blessing referring not only to that immediate future event but also, by virtue of the command of repetition, to an extended future. The entire ritual action, then, is not only cultic but also prophetic in character, first insofar as the symbolic gestures put in motion the historical events that God immediately brings about the next day (the escape from slavery, Jesus' crucifixion). This means, however, that, in celebrating the communion sacrifice, subsequent generations do not somehow reenact or repeat the singular historical event; rather, their remembrance recounts the prophetic prefiguration of that event, whose symbols were "pregnant with the future"[42] of those generations' celebrations, of their lives as a people together in communion with this God, and of the still awaited fulfillment of the reign of God anticipated by the meal.

The continuity between the structures of the meal rituals depicted in Exodus and the Last Supper accounts bespeak the fundamental Christian belief in the single God whose purpose in creation and redemption is the thriving of people in covenant with him. The radical difference, nonetheless, lies in the prepositional object added to the end of the Christian anamnesis: remembrance is kept "of me," that is, of Jesus. To "proclaim the Lord's death" by eating this bread and drinking the cup (1 Cor 11:26) is to be drawn into Jesus himself, the entire life and person who gave fully of himself in that final act.

> The symbols ordering Israel's life and hope were redrawn, focusing now upon Jesus himself. The final meal which he celebrated with his followers was not, in that sense, free-standing. It gained its significance from his own entire life and agenda, and from the events which, he knew, would shortly come to pass. It was Jesus' chosen way of investing those imminent events with the significance he believed they would carry.[43]

In the Passover context of that meal Jesus was identifying himself in the bread and cup not only as known in his words and deeds, but those as carrying forward the gifts of creation and God's unfailing covenant love to Israel and, through them, to all nations. In the Semitic world, bread signifies food as needed by humans to live. Moreover, "in the context of the Passover, bread suggests the good will of Yahweh toward his special people and therefore his constant presence."[44] The cup, containing the "fruit of the vine," signifies the Creator's gifts through the productive land but, when raised as in a toast (blessing), it also symbolizes shared love and friendship. In the context of the festive meal, it functions as a sacrifice of thanksgiving, a brimming cup of salvation, as in the psalms, celebrating "communion with the God of the covenant, with him who is himself said to be the 'cup' that is Israel's lot."[45]

Done now as memorial (anamnesis) of *Jesus*, the taking, blessing, and sharing of bread and cup is the ritual means of the absent (risen, ascended) Christ's presence as life sustenance, life itself, as life in the new covenant, empowering participants for a shared love in service "until he comes" (1 Cor 11:26). Alien to dualistic philosophies that divide body and soul, the Semitic heritage of ritual remembrance engages participants integrally, such that memory poses not the problem of how people can connect to a past event but rather the challenge of how to live the reality the commemoration actualizes among them.

Eucharistic Prayer: Transformative Power in Word and Spirit

During the first several centuries of the common era, Christianity developed alongside the rabbinic forms of Judaism that were likewise emerging in the wake of the Roman destruction of Jerusalem and the Temple in 70 CE.[46] The Syrian church-order collection called the *Didache*, conservatively dated to the early second century but now largely agreed as coming from the first, contains instruction for celebrating the Eucharist that correspond to the three steps of the supper in Luke: "He took a cup....He took bread....After supper."[47] This is, as we saw previously, the Jewish cultic prayer pattern for a festive meal or communion sacrifice in this period. Moreover, the *Didache*'s prayer texts for each of those ritual steps comprise brief *berakoth* for the first two and then, for the last, a lengthy narrative *berakah* replete with remembrance (of what God has done in Jesus), supplication (for the safety, unity, and holiness of the church and the coming of the kingdom), and doxological praise. The blessings thank God for the gifts of creation and for the "holy vine of David," that is, for Israel, from which follow the remembrance of Jesus, the supplication for the present church, and the eschatological invocation of the coming kingdom. The prayer closes with *Maranatha*, an Aramaic term that, depending on its inflection, can mean either "The Lord has come," or "Come, Lord!"[48] Thus, the prayer suggests the already/ not yet reality the church experienced, sharing in the life of the Messiah while, in the Eucharist, celebrating also the anticipation of the full coming of God's reign in him.

Andrea Bieler and Luise Schottroff explain the implications of the fact that the *Didache* belongs to a non-Jewish environment:

> The text reveals the existence of Christian communities that were not Jewish in origin and yet were thoroughly rooted in Jewish tradition. They regard themselves as those who have come to Israel through God's grace, a community who take nothing away from Israel and inherit nothing. The "holy vine of David" has been revealed to the community through Jesus (9:2)....As we already saw when we discussed the covenant theology of the early Christian Eucharist,[49] the Gentile church at this time was not seen to be separated from Israel in any negative sense. It has received honorary membership....Jesus Messiah has shown it the way to the God of Israel. Israel's ancient hope for the healing of the community of nations is expressed again here.[50]

Thus, the document is a treasure in the way it conveys both how some early Christians followed Jesus' command, "Do this in memory of me," and how as the mission spread quickly among Gentiles, the Jewish character of both the prayer and the messianic reign of God could not be dispensed with, even if tensions between the nascent church and emergent rabbinic Judaism had already begun to flare up.

The other early voice we have for the Eucharist is Justin, a Palestinian from a Greek pagan family who eventually converted to Christianity and became a prolific writer and defender of Christianity for some thirty years before his martyrdom in Rome in 165. Only two of his writings survive, one of which, found in fragments, is the oldest known Christian apology (or defense) against Judaism, a mid-second-century witness to what would gradually become a "supersessionist"[51] understanding of the church in relation to Judaism. Shortly before composing that tract, however, Justin wrote to the emperor his *First Apology*, which defends the reasonableness of Christianity and also includes descriptions of baptism and the Eucharist. Justin speaks of the assembly of the church, one person presiding, a lector proclaiming readings from the apostles and prophets, the president exhorting all to imitate what they have heard, and then all the faithful standing to offer prayers. He continues:

> When the prayers have concluded, we greet one another with a kiss. Then bread and a cup containing water and wine are brought to him who presides over the assembly. He takes these and then gives praise and glory to the Father of all things through the name of his Son and of the Holy Spirit. He offers thanks at considerable length for our being counted worthy to receive these things at his hands. When the presider has concluded these prayers and the thanksgiving, all present express their consent by saying "Amen." In Hebrew this word means "so be it." And after the presider and all the people have given their consent, those whom we call deacons give to each of those present a portion of the eucharistic bread and wine and water and take the same to those who are absent.[52]

Thus within a few Christian generations we have an account of the Eucharist that resonates with the features of Luke's Emmaus story: presider (in the story, Jesus), assembly (disciples in Luke), unfolding of the scriptures, and the table ritual of taking, blessing, breaking, and sharing. Justin continues with a straightforward explanation of what the community believes in doing this:

> We call this food the "Eucharist." No one is permitted to partake of it except those who believe that the things we teach are true and who have been washed in the bath for the forgiveness of sins and unto rebirth and who live as Christ directed. We do not receive these as if they were ordinary bread and ordinary drink, but just as Jesus our Savior was made of flesh through God's word and assumed flesh and blood for our salvation, so also the food over which the thanksgiving has been said becomes the flesh and blood of Jesus who was made flesh, doing so to nourish and transform our own flesh and blood.[53]

As we saw earlier, here again is the ancient Mediterranean/Semitic holistic understanding of the human person in motion: the eucharistic flesh and blood of Christ transforms the bodies of the baptized, empowering them to "live as Christ directed." This they do, Justin goes on to explain, by living in unity, offering mutual instruction, and helping the needy.

For all that wealth of information, Justin nonetheless leaves various aspects of the ritual vague,[54] not the least of which is the lengthy "prayers and thanksgiving" the president says over the bread and cup. Fragments of two Eastern anaphoras from the third century exist. Only from the fourth century forward do we have complete extant eucharistic prayers, which largely sustain the basic thanksgiving-petition structure of the long Jewish *berakoth*, recast in terms of Christ Jesus, while nonetheless demonstrating much variation in the details of their anamneses, supplications, and doxologies. The sacramental dimension of the eucharistic action comes through an increasingly formalized anamnesis, "which expresses the 'today' of the mystery being commemorated: the bread and wine become sacraments of the self-offering of the dead and risen Christ."[55] Here again we find variety in this element, with the offering-in-remembrance often including not only commemoration of the saving acts of Jesus in the past but also an expectant reminder of the promised future coming of Christ. As for the supplication or petitioning of divine power, the part of the prayer called the *epiclesis*, ancient churches invoked in a few cases the Messiah or the Word, while others beseeched either the Son or the Father to send the Spirit to abide in the gifts and, in many cases, the assembled church sharing them.[56] By the end of this period throughout the churches (although not in the Roman Canon) the power the epiclesis invoked on gifts and people was that of the Holy Spirit, the divine agent of creation and bodily transformation.[57]

In analyzing the eucharistic prayers in this period (the fourth to eighth centuries) we must keep in mind the trinitarian and christological controversies through which the church only gradually arrived at creedal consensuses in ecumenical councils. Even then, the decisions of the councils at Nicaea, Constantinople, and Chalcedon were called symbols and used as standards rather than as set formulas to be recited word for word in each local church's liturgy. The orthodox consensus about the persons and power of Father, Son, and Spirit, nonetheless, gradually found expression in the eucharistic prayers of the churches embracing it. At the same time, the ritual environment in which local churches celebrated the rites necessarily shifted from large houses (as late as the third century) to basilicas, a style of public building used for administering justice, political assemblies, and other civic or social gatherings. The basic structure was a vast rectangular space with rows of interior columns supporting the roof and, often, a semicircular apse at one end, where was seated the presiding officer or judge. In the case of the church, the apse became the location of the presiding minister (bishop), altar table, and reading table (ambo), all facing the assembly. While much variety in details of design and decoration evolved markedly between East and West, the overall impact of an increasingly imperial-style space, vesture, and ritual gestures inevitably affected how people experienced and understood the Eucharist.

The history going forward from the early church into subsequent periods up to modernity is, of course, complex and fraught with controversies, many divisive, as could only be the case given how central and powerful a ritual the Eucharist is in a social-cultural-political entity as wide reaching as Christianity. My purpose in this chapter, however, has been to focus on the primordial sources for the church's belief in and celebration of the real, abiding presence of Christ in the sacrament of the Eucharist, and this so as to get at the purpose for the rite: the transformation of its participants as members of Christ's Body. In the following, final chapter I consider how Christ's liturgical presence is experienced in the persons ministering to the assembly for their celebration of word and sacrament.

Chapter Four

Leadership for Christ's Body
Liturgy and Ministry

Christ's Body: A Priestly and Prophetic People

The purpose of the Eucharist is to nourish the faith of believers through the celebration of word and sacrament. In the liturgy, the content of Christ's healing, life-giving Good News comes alive and is shared as an intimate, abiding presence at table among them. The fundamental symbol of the eucharistic liturgy is the gathering of the assembly itself as the hidden presence of the risen and ascended Christ coming to light. Christ's body becomes visible in the members who assemble to participate in the paschal mystery as the Spirit-filled mission of their own lives in the world. The Eucharist is the visible manifestation of the church as Christ's Body, as the people anointed in baptism with the same Spirit who created Jesus' body in Mary's womb, possessed him uniquely through his mission unto death, and raised him bodily as the source of life for all who believe. Thus is the church the sacrament of Christ, and this most manifestly in the ritual sharing of his body and blood, the explicit priestly activity that reveals both Christ Jesus as the sole mediator between humanity and God and the community of the faithful as the priestly people acting in his name. The Eucharist is the source and summit of Christians' lives as an ongoing "living sacrifice," the "spiritual worship" (Rom 12:1) whereby they seek to make of their work, love, relationships, and social involvements an offering to the glory of the God who has made it all possible, the one who has "first loved us" (1 John 4:19). So often this priestly dimension of Christian life is not explicitly realized in the moment but only upon reflection. The sacrificial meal of the Eucharist, shaped by the word of God and animated by the Spirit, is the explicitly priestly act most revelatory of what we often might miss, the union of humans with divinity in mutual service and friendship that is the inbreaking of the kingdom of God.

Christ Jesus is the anointed king over that reign, and yet to speak thus of him is, as ever with the mystery of faith, to invoke a metaphor. For Christ is not literally a king in human history or society. As his dialogue with Pilate in John's passion account makes clear, Jesus' kingship "is not from this world" (John 18:36). And yet Christian tradition had to enlist such worldly and religious titles as *priest, prophet*, and *king* as adequate metaphors for the unique intercessory, instructive, and guiding power his Spirit now exercises among humans. In his historical life, Jesus, a Galilean layman, was a Jewish prophet in the lineage of the great classical prophets (Isaiah, Jeremiah, Ezekiel, and so forth), who themselves found in their call to confront political figures and forces a transposition in the sacrificial character of Israel's vocation. The book of the prophet Micah encapsulates the ethical turn that the prophetic tradition brought to the cultic, priestly dimension for the Jewish religion:

> "With what shall I come before the LORD,
>> and bow myself before God on high?
> Shall I come before him with burnt offerings,
>> with calves a year old?
> Will the LORD be pleased with thousands of rams,
>> with ten thousands of rivers of oil?
> Shall I give my firstborn for my transgression,
>> the fruit of my body for the sin of my soul?"
> He has told you, O mortal, what is good:
>> and what does the LORD require of you
> but to do justice, and to love kindness,
>> and to walk humbly with your God? (Mic 6:6–8)

God's message through the prophets was not that prayer and action, liturgy and ethics, or mysticism and social concern are opposed activities but, rather, that these are mutually informing practices of religious faith. The cultic and testamentary traditions of the Last Supper, as we saw in chapter 3, portray how Jesus understood the sacrificial meal he was bequeathing to his disciples as the ritual means of their participation in his life of self-giving service unto death. The Eucharist does this for Christians, revealing and empowering the identity, conscious self-awareness, and mission of the church as the sacrament of Christ, the Spirit-filled bodies participating in his grace, now in the world. And so the New Testament letters abound with language of the church as members of Christ,[1] Christians as God's holy temple in which God's Spirit dwells (see 1 Cor 3:16). Jesus, through the mystery of his death and resurrection, is the sole mediator of that Spirit (see John 16:7). The metaphor of priest, then, applies fittingly to him, as it does likewise to the people infused with his Spirit, whose lives are to be Christlike, a living sacrifice of praise.

The entire life of the church, communally and in each of its members, is a call from God, the vocation to be a priestly and prophetic body empowered with the Spirit's gifts to live out that call in faith, hope, and love. But as we saw in chapter 1, there is a hidden and scattered quality to the church's vocation in its members, who witness to God's reign (the kingdom) in diverse social roles and locations, as well as in the fact that the scope of the kingdom exceeds that of the church. As a social body itself, then, the church has, from the start, needed leadership in order to form and sustain its members in their corporate mission in the world, with leadership of the Sunday Eucharist, the ritual uniting the faithful in communion with God, among the most important roles. Here the Eucharist's central ritual power in the church comes to the fore. For the Sunday Eucharist unifies and sacramentalizes (makes visibly present) the myriad "spiritual sacrifices" (Rom 12:1) of people's daily lives in a way that keeps them in communion as one in Christ (see John 17:11), obedient to the

97

Gospel, rather than subject to the vicissitudes of human opinions, desires, and powers.

Priestly Ministry: Lessons from History

The Holy Spirit is the assurance of the Father's keeping the friends of his glorified Son in his truth (see John 15:26). From the start, this entailed that the Spirit gave gifts—*charisms* being the term derived from the original Greek of the New Testament—to individuals to serve the whole Body of Christ, the church. Not the least of these charisms were those in service to the body as a whole, to its order, to its cohesion, and to its continuity with the faith of Jesus passed down from the original apostolic (missionary) generation. The need for such leadership was (and remains) not only a human reality, insofar as Christian communities grew in size and complexity, but also a theological one, insofar as the church realizes its identity and vocation most pointedly in the Eucharist, a cultic activity itself in need of symbolic, ritual leadership. While we have no detailed information on who in the early Christian communities presided at the Eucharist and how, it seems that prophets performed this role in Syria, while structures of leadership comprised of presbyters (elders) or bishops (overseers, supervisors) or a combination thereof became widespread from the second century forward. By the third century the general pattern was for each local church to have one *episcopos* (bishop) governing the community, leading prayer, and supervising a host of other ministers, notably presbyters, who also led prayer and oversaw community needs, and deacons, who cared for the poor, prisoners, widows, and others in need.[2]

The overlap of pastoral and governing leadership with liturgical presidency, as Bernard Cooke and Gary Macy argue in their survey of early Christian polity, seemed a natural development. Assurance of the continuity of each community with Jesus became a matter of that local church being able to trace the lineage of its teachers back to those who were in the company of Jesus himself, with that lineage attesting to the legitimacy and authenticity of the current bishop.

> In this way, Christian *episcopos* in particular became the living bearers of the tradition. Possibly also they would have been chosen not only because they could remember the tradition but also because they could read the writings of the followers of Jesus. Few people could read or write, so it would be essential that at least someone in the community be able to do so. It would make sense that this person also be one of the presbyters if not the *episcopos*. If they could read, it also meant that they could lead the community in the reading and explication of scripture that was an important part of the weekly prayer services. The usual person to train those interested in becoming Christians, as well as to lead the initiation rites by which they were welcomed into the community, would be the presbyter or the *episcopos* who led the community. This meant that the leader of the community would have a central liturgical role.[3]

Along with this emerging pattern of leadership both of the local church community and its liturgical worship in the third century, these leaders began to refer to the person presiding at the rites as a "priest" (*hiereus* in Greek, *sacerdos* in Latin). This use of the term, however, referred narrowly to the symbolic role performed by the minister in leading the execution of the Eucharist and other rites (for example, baptism, initiation), a metaphor for the function of the presiding minister within the entire ritual's participation in the mystery of Christ's once-and-for-all Passover. For example, the fourth-century Syrian presbyter Theodore (later bishop of Mopsuestia) catechized, quoting heavily from the Letter to the Hebrews, that the bishop presiding at the Eucharist is a representative (*eikon*, "icon") of the one true priest, Christ Jesus, who exercises an eternal heavenly priesthood raising up all the members of the church in worship.[4]

Ordination ceremonies for bishops from early on generally followed the pattern whereby the ministers of the local church chose someone to be endorsed by the entire community, with bishops from the wider area laying hands on the man as a symbol of the universal (catholic) church's acceptance and approval. By the fifth century, bishops functioned as relatively independent leaders of their churches (or dioceses), with patriarchs of the largest churches functioning as regional leaders and councils serving as the mechanism for bishops to gather for decisions about issues of faith and order affecting the universal church. Thus, the office of bishop had become quite established through a pattern that developed over those first centuries. From the fourth into the fifth century, however, the new development was an increasingly sharp distinction between the clergy and the laity (the body of the faithful) by attributing to the ordained a priestly status akin to that of the temple priesthood of Israel.

In a "radical departure from the New Testament notion of the priestly body of Christ,"[5] the title of priest no longer functioned only within the symbolic action of the Eucharist (or other sacraments) but rather became constitutive of the status of bishop and presbyter. With this shift came the association of sacrificial ritual leadership with strict purity laws, such that presbyters were not to have sexual relations with their wives prior to celebrating the Eucharist. As the practice of daily Mass evolved in the West, this eventually amounted to priests not being able to have sex at all and, indeed, in the twelfth century celibacy became mandatory for the ordained. That decision coincided with the medieval West's waning appreciation for the symbolic power of the sacraments as communal celebrations, such that the presence and efficacy of Christ's sacrifice was a matter of an objective reality presented by the priest, who silently prayed the canon, to the onlooking people.[6] The ordained were literally priests, in the ancient Jewish or even pagan senses of the term (intermediaries with sacred powers), with their meaning and purpose "'ordered' primarily to the celebration of the Eucharist rather than to communal or pastoral leadership. It is in part this sacralization of Christian life to which the Reformers of the sixteenth century objected."[7] To the Reformation's recovery of the priestly character of all the faithful and the central role of teaching and proclamation for the ordained, the Catholic Counter-Reformation reacted with an even narrower focus on the priest's power to confect the sacraments, especially the body and blood of Christ on the altar.

Only with the Second Vatican Council in the 1960s did Roman Catholicism begin to recover a balanced, scripturally and traditionally informed approach to ordained ministry, placing primary emphasis on the proclamation of the word of God in conjunction with cultic power and ecclesial leadership.[8] This theological and pastoral breakthrough has afforded bilateral discussions with major Protestant denominations and Eastern Orthodoxy, who themselves have also been in mutual ecumenical dialogues. A convergence in theological understanding is evident in the World Council of Churches' 1982 Faith and Order document, which wisely asserts the calling of all the baptized as the basis for particular ministries: "The chief responsibility of the ordained ministry is to assemble and build up the Body of Christ by proclaiming and teaching the Word of God, by celebrating the sacraments, and by guiding the life of the community in its worship, its mission and its caring ministry."[9] Still, serious divisions remain. The nature and authority of ordained ministry persists as one of the most challenging obstacles to unity, especially concerning what constitutes apostolic succession, that is, the question of how the permanence and continuity of the first witnesses to Christ is embodied by bishops and their presbyters.[10] This is sadly ironic, given ordained ministry's traditional function of unifying the church, on both the local and universal levels. The history and present state of these problems reach far beyond the scope of this present chapter, but that does not preclude our benefiting from the ecumenical advances theological scholarship has made concerning Christ's presence in ministry to word and sacrament, especially in the Eucharist.

Liturgical Presidency:
Sacrament within a Sacrament

If *Baptism, Eucharist and Ministry* presents an unflinching acknowledgment of the gravity and extent of the problems entailed in the lack of mutual recognition of ministries and common understanding of apostolic succession among churches, it nonetheless attests to the near-universal recognition of the need for ordained ministry:

> It is especially in the Eucharistic celebration that the ordained ministry is the visible focus of the deep and all-embracing communion between Christ and the members of his body. In the celebration of the eucharist, Christ gathers, teaches, and nourishes the church. It is Christ who invites to the meal and who presides at it. In most churches this presidency is signified and represented by an ordained minister.[11]

Once again we hear echoes of the church's primordial story of its eucharistic celebration, Luke's Easter afternoon account of Christ with the disciples on the Emmaus road. It is the risen Christ who directs the entire action, coming to form them as companions who receive the word of redemption and share a communion with him they could never have imagined. Scripture reveals the church's need, as a communal body, for a unifying leadership of the entire ritual action, one that is personal and charismatic (Spirit filled) so as to symbolize (signify, represent) the Lord Jesus. In leading the assembled Body of Christ in the sacramental celebration of their priestly mission, the ordained minister—called the priest in many churches—pronounces the prayer of the liturgy "in the name of Christ," such that all hear and respond to it as the "the word of Christ himself."[12] Christian priests are not intermediaries at the altar, as in the ancient Jewish temple or pagan cults; rather, they "sacramentally manifest, in virtue of the sacrament of holy orders which they have received, the unique mediation of Christ in whose name they preside."[13] The community needs the presiding ordained minister, the priest, for the ordering of their priestly celebration, that is, a powerful sensory manifestation of the divine Spirit of Christ's active presence in their lives and world through the symbolic media of word, sacrament, and the assembly of the people themselves.

The presence of Christ in the ordained minister, as Bernard Cooke has argued consistently throughout his historical and theological scholarship, emerges through that person's gifted and exemplary service to the Christian community's mission of sharing the life of God's reign, signaling the very goal of God's creative purpose in the world. "The ordained person is not the grace-giver, in sole possession of the 'magical' power, but a sacrament (of the great church's faith) within a sacrament."[14] The presider serves the common priesthood of the liturgical assembly: "Those who belong to this special ministerial group are not more priestly than other Christians, but they are called to give special sacramental expression to Christ's priestly action of Passover so that the entire community can celebrate more authentically and fully its priestly character."[15] One of the key ways the ordained presider authenticates and enhances the entire action of the liturgy is by endowing it with a sense of divine constancy and the continuity of the community's celebration with the apostolic tradition of the church. Another lies in the competence, knowledge, and personal qualities brought by the priest-presider to the celebration of the rites, thereby serving all the ways in which Christ is present and active in the celebration. Both of these points warrant some elaboration.

As with the notion of the sacramental character of baptism,[16] ordination should not be understood as an individual possession but in a corporate sense, signifying that "God is the one who initiates and sustains all sacramental relationships" in the church.[17] As the possession not of the individual minister but a gift (charism) of the Holy Sprit for edification of the ecclesial body,[18] ordination affirms that God is utterly faithful to the church and its members, regardless of how much Christians may struggle or falter. The New Testament and early church fathers give ample evidence that the building up of the life of the community was the priority and goal of the charisms (Spirit-gifts) and leadership in the nascent church.[19] The church in all generations, then, has an "apostolic right" to ministry, "its evangelical right to the pastoral leadership that has been given by God."[20] Through the church's recognition in the ordination ritual of the priestly minister's charism and mission "without reserve or time limit,"[21] the presider at Eucharist signifies to the church and world that all ministry is God's work and not merely a matter of human motivation.

Theological seminary training and apostolic experiments (or pastoral trials), building on candidates' gifts, are the primary way today's local churches (dioceses or conferences) assure that the people they ordain for pastoral-liturgical ministry are bearers of the apostolic tradition.

> Apostolic tradition in the Church means continuity in the permanent characteristics of the Church of the apostles: witness to the apostolic faith, proclamation and fresh interpretation of the Gospel, celebration of baptism and the eucharist, the transmission of ministerial responsibilities, communion in prayer, love, joy and suffering, service to the sick and the needy, unity among the local churches and sharing the gifts which the Lord has given to each.[22]

Genuine Christian leaders are those whose lives are so Spirit filled as to be instruments of grace (sacraments) to others, whose words and deeds are evidence of the "consecration" of their lives to God.[23] Such consecration does not, Cooke insists, derive from office, nor is it limited to those who hold office. Rather, the lives and ministerial work of the ordained need to be of such an apostolic quality as to lead and empower the community's gifts in service to one another and the world. Through "visible acts of caring" in various ministries the risen Christ is made present among people, which presence "is celebrated in all the rituals over which [ordained] ministers preside, but particularly in the Sunday service."[24]

The priestly and prophetic work of ordained ministry requires a deep knowledge of scripture, especially for homiletic preaching, and of the ritual's traditional symbols, so as both to preside over them and to enable a range of liturgical ministries in service to the community's celebration. The presider's ministry is first and foremost prayerful, as the entire liturgical action is the great prayer of the church. In this the iconic nature of the presider's ministry emerges as the person whose words and actions at once embody the assembly's "'calling out' and 'raising up in offering'" to God and Christ's "'gathering' and 'associating' the people of the Church in his own worship of *Abba*."[25] Presidential ministry serves as both the focal point of all the actions and movements comprising the liturgy and the orchestrator of the other ministries that proclaim the word, serve and sustain the assembly as a unified body of prayer, and support the eucharistic act of offering and communion. The final task for this chapter, then, is to consider briefly the various ministries in relation to their function within the entire "space" of the liturgy. This may also serve as a concluding appreciation for how communion in Christ's paschal mystery comes about concretely through the whole range of the liturgy's symbolism and ritual action.

Liturgical Ministries: Shaping the Liturgy's Space

Liturgy is a work (*-urgy*, from the Greek, *ergon*) that takes place in time and space. The rhythm of the eucharistic liturgy's time is founded on Sunday as the Lord's Day, the Day of the Resurrection, the Eighth Day of creation opening toward the full realization of the kingdom of God.[26] The liturgy's space is comprised of every and all physical constituents of the action, of which the most fundamental are the people themselves, the assembled body of the local church under the leadership of their ordained presiding minister. Everything else about the space is configured to what the People of God need in order to perform the services of word and table so as to encounter the crucified and risen Christ in ways that reveal and confirm his presence and action in their lives. The Second Vatican Council put it well in its famous and oft-quoted programmatic statement: "The faithful should be led to that full, conscious, and active participation in liturgical celebrations which is demanded by the very nature of the liturgy, and to which the Christian people, 'a chosen race, a royal priesthood, a holy nation, a redeemed people' (1 Pet. 2:9, 4—5) have a right and obligation by reason of their baptism."[27] As we saw in the case of ordained ministry, all the ministries that serve the participation of the faithful in the liturgy find their source in baptism, with its call to live the Good News as an invitation from God empowered with the particular gifts formed by Christ's Spirit in each. When elicited for the practical execution but also beautiful inspiration of the liturgy, human talents for public speaking and reading, music and the arts, organization and hospitality prove to be charisms that individuals exercise for building up the Body of Christ.

Fundamental to the space for celebration are the stable furnishings in the sanctuary: the altar table for the sacrificial meal, the ambo for the proclamation of God's word, and the presidential chair signifying the ordained minister's leadership function in the name of Christ. Stable features also include the seating arrangements for the assembly and situation of the musicians, allowing for good sight lines and acoustics as well as free movement, and a comfortable and welcoming entry area with the baptismal font usually located on the threshold between the entry and the main assembly space. All of these physical elements of the liturgical space symbolically locate ministries for the good, if not beautiful and inspiring, participation of all in the celebration of word and sacrament. While perhaps drawing the least attention or personal recognition, the ministries entailed in preparing the sanctuary and entire space and, more remotely, the design and installation of all the spatial features themselves, are essential contributions to the church's liturgical worship. Sacristans require knowledge of the material elements and movements of the rites as they work behind the scenes before and after services, while more proximate to the assembling people are greeters, who distribute printed worship aids and welcome strangers and guests to the community's gathering. None of these quiet works around the edges of the celebration should be underestimated; indeed, the Gospels and New Testament letters give ample indication of the reign of God emerging in the seemingly least acts of service in the name of the Lord.

Moving to the opening rites entails attention to sound and silence, positioning and posture. Of irreducible value, and therefore necessity, to uniting the people as one body at the outset of the liturgy is music.[28] While a prelude on organ or other instruments attunes human ears, and thereby each individual body, to vibrations that produce common sounds among them, the opening hymn or song orients each person horizontally amid the assembly and vertically to God. The posture is one of standing, an anthropological sign of respect and attentiveness that bears the theological significance of paschal joy and dignity for those assembled in Christ, as well as eschatological expectation of the Lord's return. Combined with standing, the activities of singing and hearing heighten each person's bodily and mental awareness of coming into an encounter with God. The tones and overtones of the hymn and its accompaniment within, around, and above the human bodies at worship draw people's consciousness "upward." Furthermore, participation in the gathering song orients each person horizontally within the body of the assembly, the Body of Christ. Here the function is one of unifying the group as a corporate body of action. For "by its rhythm and melody [song] produces such a fusion of voices that there seems to be but a single singer. As a matter of fact, once there is a question of more than a small group of people, song alone makes it possible for an assembly to express itself as one."[29] The assembled serve one another by producing the tones and overtones of their singing, not only neurologically stimulating each person's mind and body but also achieving a certain synchrony among their bodies as their heartbeats and breath align with the rhythm, pulse, and pace of the music. The point here is that liturgical music is a matter not only of cognition, through the content and meaning of the words in hymn texts, but also of somatic stimulation and synchrony physically uniting the assembled body of believers.

Given the functional purpose of music in the liturgy, music ministry clearly is not about entertainment or covering over silences or gaps in the order of service but rather providing forms of music in rhythm with the services of word and table that lead people into the heart of the paschal mystery.[30] The first responsibility of music ministers is to foster a participatory attitude in the worshiping community and to build a repertoire of hymns, psalms, and chants, through repetition, that is suitable to the assembly's aptitude and particular cultural-ecclesial heritage or tradition.[31] The music director must be knowledgeable of the seasons of the church year and the content of the lectionary cycle, as scripture is as foundational for this aspect of the liturgy as any other. During the service itself the assembly needs leadership in song, which usually is provided by at least a cantor and often a choir, suitably positioned in relation to the congregation so that the director or cantor can help the assembly with their parts. As in any good musical performance, the accompanying musicians must be attentive to the singing being supported while also providing whatever measure of artistry possible. The celebration needs the sound not only of music but also of silence, allowing the divine Spirit and human bodies to breathe, such that the acoustical space may be genuinely prayerful. Much more could be said, and has been written, on this entirely important dimension of the church's worship. Finally notable, however, is the role of the psalmist, that is, the minister who from the ambo, the place for the proclamation of God's word, leads the assembly in chanting the psalm that the lectionary pairs with the first reading in the service of the word. The psalms are liturgical songs whose meaning and power become an event of God's revelatory word when chanted or sung, whether antiphonally or responsorially, by cantor and congregation.

As with ministry to the liturgy's music, the service of lectors or readers is not a mere ritual function but rather a call to personal, prayerful engagement with and sufficient knowledge of the content of the scriptures. Such immersion in the biblical word of God serves the assembly's need to hear that word come alive in their midst, with the reader nonetheless also taking into account the acoustical qualities (and sometimes, challenges) of the worship space. In most churches one or two lectors proclaim the first and second readings during the service of the word, while the presider or some other ordained minister proclaims the Gospel reading and preaches the homily. The latter is itself a proclamation of the word, opening the meaning of the scriptures for the assembly in the present moment, and thus requires both extensive biblical-theological education and the church's ordination of the minister so that the people might confidently expect to hear Christ's Spirit speaking through the words. The assembly's response is to bring the needs of the church and world to the saving Christ who has come in the proclaimed word, with either a deacon or lay reader pronouncing the intercessory prayers and the faithful adding their spoken or chanted formula of petition to each (for example, "Lord, have mercy" or "Hear us, O God").

The liturgy's movement into the service of the Eucharist activates the work of acolytes or altar servers, one or more of whom would have led the presider and other ministers in the entrance procession and assisted the presider by holding the sacramentary or ritual book. The servers (and sometimes a deacon) help prepare the table for the eucharistic prayer, assisting the priest-presider in receiving the gifts of bread and wine from a procession of the faithful. A server also prepares the thurible, should incense be used as an enhancement of the visual and olfactory beauty of the offering and a symbol of the people's dignity and ascending prayer. These elements, as well as candles and often a processional crucifix borne by acolytes or servers at this and other points in the liturgy, contribute richly to the liturgical space and the festive solemnity of the paschal celebration. By wearing white albs in the service, these assisting ministers represent the white robe all received at baptism (while the ordained put on further symbols of office over that basic baptismal garment). During the communion rite, deacons, acolytes, or other designated ministers usually assist with the distribution of the eucharistic bread and wine to the people, while a processional hymn helps unify the faithful (by the same somatic dynamics as in the entrance hymn) so as to support the tangible experience of sharing as one in the body and blood of Christ.

All the elements of rite involved in the assembly's celebration of word and sacrament in the eucharistic liturgy, including the various ministers, are irreducible symbolic means for the members of Christ's Body to encounter and be nourished as a church and sent forth to continue their lives as spiritual sacrifices. Renewed in body and spirit with Christ's food for the journey, the people are dismissed in blessing and peace to witness by lives of faith to the glory of God and for the salvation of the world.

Conclusion

By ending with consideration of how ministries in the assembly create and sustain the space of the liturgical celebration, chapter 4 brought our study of Christ's presence in the Eucharist full circle. For the crucified and risen Lord's sacramental presence is *in* and *for* the church. Eliciting ancient tradition, such eminent theologians in our time as the Jesuit Henri de Lubac and the Orthodox John Zizioulas have opened up the implications of the fathers' teachings on how the liturgy is not so much first a matter of the church making the Eucharist as the Eucharist making the church.[1] The Eucharist reveals God to us in Christ Jesus, reveals the humanity of God (as the one who is for us), reveals the paschal mystery of Christ's death and resurrection as a continuous offer of sharing in divine life as creative and redemptive life for the world. Situated in the ongoing history of this world, such sharing takes place only in real communities of faith, local churches assembled at specific times and in particular places.

Liturgical theologians, therefore, are wont to point out that the performance of liturgy, that is, the actual practice of the rites, is *primary theology*. Books such as the present one are *secondary theology*, an exercise already one step removed from the first order of the church's work, namely, actual celebrations of the liturgy.[2] In the doing of the liturgy people respond to the divine invitation to encounter the living Christ as their life, as the truth of God's word written on their bodies, as the way their lives are joined to the mission of God's reign of justice, mercy, and peace among people. The multivalent symbolism of the Eucharist—the ritual activity of

111

assembling, being addressed apostolically in the name of Christ, hearing and responding to the word of God, and communing in divine presence through creaturely gifts of bread and wine— inspires believers' thoughts and imaginations according to the character of Christ's Spirit.

For a modern humanity prone to identifying scientific or physical evidence as the singular measure of truth, philosopher Paul Ricoeur recovered the fundamental meaning-making activity of symbolism in his oft-quoted maxim: The symbol gives rise to thought, and thought returns to the symbol.[3] The church experiences this human process as sacramental, as revelatory of the divine mystery of faith. Believers of all ages and ranges of intellectual acumen reflect upon their eucharistic experiences in any number of ways (individually, communally, institutionally) and moments (instantaneously and over time) to attain to the Christ-meaning of life and death in the real world of symbols. The ongoing dialogue between participation in the liturgy and ethical engagement in daily life and wider society comprise the primary word from and to God in the Body of Christ's members, the church. In that sense, then, every believer, to the extent one engages in such symbolic and ethical action inspiring reflection, and reflection inspiring action, is a practical theologian.

The vocation of the professional theologian is for service to that dialogical process of the church's life in its members through a learned and sustained engagement in thought as it arises from and returns to the symbols of lived faith. It is within that framework that the present book offers itself as a resource for practicing the Eucharist today. Guiding what I hope might prove to readers a refreshing approach to the Eucharist as encounter with the crucified and risen Christ has been the conviction that both sound tradition and theological reflection have as their fundamental resource the Bible, the sacred scriptures of the church. Such an orientation provides for ecumenical dialogue, if not an ecumenical theology, accessible to a wide range of liturgically centered churches and Christian communities. Theological interpretation and appropriation of scripture has throughout Christian history entailed drawing upon philosophical and other literary and cultural approaches to texts, myths, narratives, and symbols current to the time and place (the era and location) in which the theologian, whether bishop or mystic or professor, operates. In the case of this present book I have availed myself of current critical biblical scholarship as such historically informed work meets the questions, challenges, and sensibilities of us late-modern believers.

Thus, I leave these chapters in the hands of readers so that thought might return to the symbol in the Eucharist, renewing believers' participation in the paschal mystery, the Word and Spirit's work of recreating us in the image and likeness of the God who raised Jesus from the dead.[4] Surely, we practice the faith's tradition in an era of great anthropological change. In these early years of a new millennium we are experiencing significant, even drastic, transformation in how humans go about being human— in relation to self and others, social institutions and natural environs. With millennia of generations gone before us, we find ourselves no less called to faith in the Christ Jesus acclaimed at the start of the Easter Vigil, that "mother of all vigils"[5] that annually renews the church's very being through baptism and the Eucharist. Inscribing ancient biblical symbols on the paschal candle, the presiding celebrant proclaims amid the assembly gathered in darkness around the primordial fire:

> Christ, yesterday and today
> the beginning and the end
> Alpha
> and Omega
> all time belongs to him
> and all the ages
> to him be glory and power
> through every age for ever. Amen.[6]

Notes

Introduction: Participating in the Mystery of Christ's Sacramental Presence

1. Louis-Marie Chauvet, *The Sacraments: The Word of God at the Mercy of the Body* (Collegeville, MN: Liturgical Press, 2001), pp. 156, 158.

2. See I. H. Dalmais, "Theology of the Liturgical Celebration," in *Principles of the Liturgy,* Vol. 1 of *The Church at Prayer,* ed. A. G. Martimort, trans. Matthew O'Connell (Collegeville, MN: Liturgical Press, 1987), p. 264.

3. *Liturgy and Tradition: Theological Reflections of Alexander Schmemann,* ed. Thomas Fisch (Crestwood, NY: St. Vladimir's Seminary Press, 1990), pp. 51–52.

4. For citations and discussion of Augustine's *City of God* 10.6 and Sermon 227, see J.-M.-R. Tillard, *Flesh of the Church, Flesh of Christ: At the Source of the Ecclesiology of Communion,* trans. Madeleine Beaumont (Collegeville, MN: Liturgical Press, 2001), pp. 47–48, 133.

5. Ibid., p. 109.

6. Friendship as fundamental symbol (sacrament) of divine love humanly experienced as grace, definitively in Jesus, has been a hallmark throughout Bernard Cooke's theological writings. For the most recent elaboration, see his *Power and the Spirit of God: Toward an Experience-Based Pneumatology* (New York: Oxford University Press, 2004), pp. 168–77.

7. See *Liturgy and Tradition,* 95–97, pp. 123–25.

8. Methodist moral theologian Stanley M. Hauerwas has critiqued the extreme form biblical fundamentalist practices can take: "They [many 'conservative' Christians], of course, say they use the name of Jesus, but they fail to see that *how* Jesus' name is used makes all the difference. Without the Eucharist, for example, we lack the means to know the kind of presence Jesus' resurrection makes possible." "Worship, Evangelism, Ethics: On Eliminating the 'And,'" in *Liturgy and the Moral Self: Humanity at Full Stretch before God*, ed. E. Byron Anderson and Bruce T. Morrill (Collegeville, MN: Liturgical Press, 1998), p. 101.

9. The Constitution on the Sacred Liturgy: *Sacrosanctum Concilium*, no. 33, accessible at http://www.vatican.va/archive/hist_ councils/ii_vatican_council/documents/vat-ii_const_19631204_ sacrosanctum-concilium_en.html.

10. Dalmais, "Theology of the Liturgical Celebration," p. 266. Father Dalmais, a Dominican friar, served for years on the faculty of the Parisian Institut Supérieur de Liturgie and was one of the scholars of the French Liturgical Movement so influential in crafting the reformed Roman Rites mandated by the Second Vatican Council.

11. Constitution on the Sacred Liturgy, no. 7.

12. Here I follow Chauvet, who establishes this story as the biblical paradigm for his sacramental-liturgical theology. See *The Sacraments*, pp. 22–31.

13. Luke 24:35. "The way" is a title for the nascent church in Luke's Acts of the Apostles (see 9:2; 19:9,23; 22:4; 24:14,22). See Raymond E. Brown, *An Introduction to the New Testament*, The Anchor Bible Reference Library (New York: Doubleday, 1997), pp. 314–15, and 287, n. 21.

14. Peter E. Fink, *Worship: Praying the Sacraments* (Washington, DC: Pastoral Press, 1991), p. 84.

15. Ibid., p. 85.

16. Ibid., p. 84.

Chapter 1: Hidden Presence

1. The Constitution on the Sacred Liturgy: *Sacrosanctum Concilium*, no. 26, accessible at http://www.vatican.va/archive/hist_councils/ii_vatican_council/documents/vat-ii_const_19631204_sacrosanctum-concilium_en.html.

2. Bernard Cooke, *Sacraments and Sacramentality*, rev. ed. (Mystic, CT: Twenty-Third Publications, 1994), pp. 73–76.

3. J.-M.-R. Tillard, *Flesh of the Church, Flesh of Christ: At the Source of the Ecclesiology of Communion*, trans. Madeleine Beaumont (Collegeville, MN: Liturgical Press, 2001), p. 33. Tillard (†2000), a Dominican friar from Canada, was a tireless ecumenist on the Faith and Order Commission of the World Council of Churches.

4. *Christian Initiation, General Introduction*, no. 2.

5. For a discussion of the patristic notion of a good but fallen creation, see *Liturgy and Tradition: Theological Reflections of Alexander Schmemann*, ed. Thomas Fisch (Crestwood, NY: St. Vladimir's Seminary Press, 1990), pp. 97–99.

6. *Baptism, Eucharist and Ministry*, Faith and Order Paper No. 111 (Geneva: World Council of Churches, 1982), pt. 1, nos. 6, 7.

7. See Constitution on the Sacred Liturgy, no. 10.

8. *Baptism, Eucharist and Ministry*, commentary on no. 14 (italics in the original).

9. *Christian Initiation, General Introduction*, no. 2.

10. See Jerome Murphy-O'Connor, "Eucharist and Community in First Corinthians," in *Living Bread, Saving Cup: Readings on the Eucharist*, ed. R. Kevin Seasoltz (Collegeville, MN: Liturgical Press, 1987), pp. 1–30. See also Bruce T. Morrill, *Anamnesis as Dangerous Memory: Political and Liturgical Theology in Dialogue* (Collegeville, MN: Liturgical Press, 2000), pp. 180–86.

11. Tillard, *Flesh of the Church, Flesh of Christ*, pp. 22–23.

12. See Nathan Mitchell, *Mission and Ministry: History and Theology in the Sacrament of Order* (Collegeville, MN: Michael Glazier/Liturgical Press, 1982), p. 235. See also Bernard Cooke,

Power and the Spirit of God: Toward an Experience-Based Pneumatology (New York: Oxford University Press, 2004), pp. 153, 171.

13. See Edward Schillebeeckx, *Christ the Sacrament of the Encounter with God* (New York: Sheed & Ward, 1963), pp. 155–56. Application of the precise terminology of "sacramental character," which followed from Augustine's explanation of the seal of baptism, attests that in the fourth and fifth centuries the lifelong reality of valid ordinations was likewise already a long-held assumption. See Bernard Cooke, *Ministry to Word and Sacraments: History and Theology* (Philadelphia: Fortress, 1976), p. 546.

14. Thomas Aquinas, *Summa Theologica*, III, q. 63, art. 2, in *Summa Theologica of St. Thomas Aquinas*, Vol. 4, trans. Fathers of the English Dominican Province (Westminster, MD: Christian Classics, 1948/1981), p. 2356.

15. III, q. 63, art. 5. Ibid., p. 2359.

16. See Cooke, *Ministry to Word and Sacraments*, p. 289.

17. The Dogmatic Constitution on the Church: *Lumen Gentium*, no. 11, accessible at http://www.vatican.va/archive/hist_councils/ii_vatican_council/documents/vat-ii_const_19641121_lumen-gentium_en.html.

18. Karl Rahner, *The Church and the Sacraments*, trans. W. J. O'Hara (Edinburgh/London: Nelson, 1963), pp. 88–89.

19. Cooke, *Ministry to Word and Sacraments*, p. 644.

20. Louis-Marie Chauvet, *The Sacraments: The Word of God at the Mercy of the Body* (Collegeville, MN: Liturgical Press, 2001), pp. 31–32.

21. Ibid., p. xv.

22. Ibid., p. 34 (emphasis in the original).

23. R. C. D. Jasper and G. J. Cuming, eds., *Prayers of the Eucharist: Early and Reformed*, 3rd ed. (Collegeville, MN: Liturgical Press, 1990), p. 29.

24. For another overview of the biblical material, with further bibliographical references, see Judith M. Kubicki, *The Presence of Christ in the Gathered Assembly* (New York: Continuum, 2006), pp. 38–40.

25. See Irénée Henri Dalmais et al., *Principles of the Liturgy*, The Church at Prayer, ed. A. G. Martimort, trans. Matthew O'Connell, Vol. 1 (Collegeville, MN: Liturgical Press, 1987), p. 92.

26. Xavier Léon-Dufour, *Sharing the Eucharistic Bread: The Witness of the New Testament*, trans. Matthew O'Connell (New York: Paulist Press, 1987), p. 145.

27. Ibid., p. 146.

28. N. T. Wright, *Jesus and the Victory of God*, Christian Origins and the Question of God, Vol. 2 (Minneapolis: Augsburg Fortress, 1996), p. 562.

29. Andrea Bieler and Luise Schottroff, *The Eucharist: Bodies, Bread, and Resurrection* (Minneapolis: Fortress, 2007), p. 22.

30. Ibid., p. 34.

31. See ibid., 206, nn. 36, 37.

32. See Léon-Dufour, *Sharing the Eucharistic Bread*, pp. 152; 355, n. 54.

33. Ibid., p. 142.

34. Ibid., p. 150.

35. See ibid., p. 153.

36. See Louis-Marie Chauvet, *Symbol and Sacrament: A Sacramental Reinterpretation of Christian Existence*, trans. Patrick Madigan and Madeleine Beaumont (Collegeville, MN: Liturgical Press, 1995), pp. 146–52. For a summary and application of Chauvet's concept of the "person-body" as a "triple-body" of nature, culture, and tradition, see Bruce T. Morrill, *Divine Worship and Human Healing: Liturgical Theology at the Margins of Life and Death* (Collegeville, MN: Liturgical Press, 2009), pp. 207, 230–40.

37. Bieler and Schottroff, *The Eucharist*, p. 25.

38. Dalmais et al., *Principles of the Liturgy*, p. 244.

39. Ibid., p. 96.

40. See Robert Cabié, *The Eucharist*, The Church at Prayer, ed. A. G. Martimort, trans. Matthew O'Connell, Vol. 2 (Collegeville, MN: Liturgical Press, 1986), pp. 191–92.

41. Ibid., 19. Such a "cost of discipleship" is experienced to this day by many Christians in Asia, as well as in certain parts of Africa.

42. See Hal Taussig, *In the Beginning Was the Meal: Social Experimentation and Early Christian Identity* (Minneapolis: Fortress, 2009), pp. 21–54.

43. "The shortest definition of religion: interruption." Johann Baptist Metz, *Faith in History and Society: Toward a Practical Fundamental Theology*, trans. J. Matthew Ashley (New York: Crossroad, 2007), p. 158.

44. See Morrill, *Anamnesis as Dangerous Memory*, pp. 26–34, 50–62.

45. Don E. Saliers, *Worship as Theology: Foretaste of Glory Divine* (Nashville: Abingdon, 1994), pp. 191–92.

46. Margaret Mary Kelleher, "The Liturgical Body: Symbol and Ritual," in *Bodies of Worship: Explorations in Theory and Practice*, ed. Bruce T. Morrill (Collegeville, MN: Liturgical Press, 1999), p. 53. In her explanation of ritual Kelleher draws on the work of Robert Grimes, Catherine Bell, and others.

47. See Louis-Marie Chauvet, "The Liturgy in Its Symbolic Space," in *Liturgy and the Body*, ed. Louis-Marie Chauvet and François Kabasele Lumbala, *Concilium* 1995/3 (London/Maryknoll: SCM /Orbis, 1995), pp. 29–39. Here I repeat the appropriation of Chauvet's theory I first published as a footnote in my introduction to *Bodies of Worship: Explorations in Theory and Practice* (Collegeville, MN: Liturgical Press, 1999), p. 7, n. 15.

Chapter 2: Holy Scripture

1. See Philip Kenneson, "Gathering: Worship, Imagination, and Formation," in *The Blackwell Companion to Christian Ethics*, ed. Stanley Hauerwas and Samuel Wells (Malden, MA/Oxford, UK: Blackwell, 2004), pp. 58–59.

2. Text: Henry Alford, 1810–71, alt. Tune: ST. GEORGE'S WINDSOR, 77 77 D; George J. Elvey, 1816–93. In *Ritual Song: A*

Hymnal and Service Book for Roman Catholics (Chicago: GIA, 1996), no. 706.

3. Mary Catherine Hilkert, *Naming Grace: Preaching and the Sacramental Imagination* (New York: Continuum, 1998), p. 61.

4. See G. W. H. Lampe, *God as Spirit* (Oxford, UK: Clarendon Press, 1977), pp. 35–37.

5. Sandra M. Schneiders, *The Revelatory Text: Interpreting the New Testament as Sacred Scripture*, 2nd ed. (Collegeville, MN: Liturgical Press, 1999), p. 34.

6. Ibid., p. 39.

7. Lucien Deiss, *Celebration of the Word*, trans. Lucien Deiss and Jane Burton (Collegeville, MN: Liturgical Press, 1993), pp. 3, 4, 21.

8. See N. T. Wright, *Jesus and the Victory of God*, Christian Origins and the Question of God, Vol. 2 (Minneapolis: Fortress, 1996), pp. 94–98, 202–9.

9. Alexander Schmemann, *Introduction to Liturgical Theology*, trans. Asheleigh Moore (Crestwood, NY: St. Vladimir's Seminary Press, 1966, 1986), pp. 79–80.

10. Andrea Bieler and Luise Schottroff, *The Eucharist: Bodies, Bread, and Resurrection* (Minneapolis: Fortress, 2007), p. 41.

11. See the Constitution on the Sacred Liturgy: *Sacrosanctum Concilium*, no. 10, accessible at http://www.vatican.va/archive/hist_councils/ii_vatican_council/documents/vat-ii_const_19631204_sacrosanctum-concilium_en.html.

12. See Gordon W. Lathrop, *Holy Things: A Liturgical Theology* (Minneapolis: Fortress, 1993), pp. 36–43.

13. Constitution on the Sacred Liturgy, no. 106.

14. See ibid., no. 51.

15. Louis-Marie Chauvet, *The Sacraments: The Word of God at the Mercy of the Body* (Collegeville, MN: Liturgical Press, 2001), p. 156.

16. See Constitution on the Sacred Liturgy, nos. 24, 35, 51.

17. Horace T. Allen, "Lectionaries," in *The New Westminster Dictionary of Liturgy and Worship*, ed. Paul Bradshaw (Louisville/London: Westminster John Knox, 2002), p. 275.

18. For details see, The Revised Common Lectionary: A Service of the Vanderbilt Divinity Library, at http://lectionary.library.vanderbilt.edu/.

19. David N. Power, *"The Word of the Lord": Liturgy's Use of Scripture* (Maryknoll, NY: Orbis, 2001), pp. 13–14. The text Power quotes is Eric Q. Gritsch and Robert W. Jenson, *Lutheranism: The Theological Movement and Its Confessional Writings* (Philadelphia: Fortress, 1976), p. 11.

20. For a more detailed outline of the history and shape of the liturgical year, see Pierre Jounel, "The Year," in *The Liturgy and Time*, The Church at Prayer, Vol. 4, ed. A. G. Martimort, trans. Matthew J. O'Connell (Collegeville, MN: Liturgical Press, 1986), pp. 33–96.

21. Introduction to the *Lectionary for Mass*, no. 60 (International Committee on English in the Liturgy, 1981).

22. Introduction to the *Lectionary for Mass*, no. 3.

23. Deiss, *Celebration of the Word*, p. 11.

24. Hilkert, *Naming Grace*, p. 138.

25. Power, *"The Word of the Lord,"* p. 14.

26. Ibid., pp. 15–16.

27. Hilkert, *Naming Grace*, p. 78.

28. Ibid., p. 81.

29. Ibid., p. 77. Hilkert provides a bibliography of pertinent writings by Sandra Schneiders, who coined the term "paschal imagination."

Chapter 3: Eucharistic Communion

1. Kevin W. Irwin, *Context and Text: Method in Liturgical Theology* (Collegeville, MN: Liturgical Press, 1994), p. 180.

2. Augustine, Sermon 272, *Patrologiae Latina*, trans. J.-P. Migne, cited in Joseph M. Powers, *Eucharistic Theology* (New York: Seabury, 1967), p. 20.

3. "The Church…, especially in the sacred liturgy,…unceasingly receives and offers to the faithful the bread of life from the table both of God's word and of Christ's body." Dogmatic Constitution on

Divine Revelation: *Dei Verbum*, no. 21, accessible at http://www. vatican.va/archive/hist_councils/ii_vatican_council/documents/vat-ii_const_19651118_dei-verbum_en.html.

4. In my attempt to capture something of the skewed notions of Christ's death as sacrifice or atonement that evolved in the wake of early Christianity I echo the work of the Swedish Lutheran theologian Gustaf Aulén, who distinguished and criticized "objectivist" and "subjectivist" models in contrast to what he championed as the ancient "classical account." The latter, Aulén argues, integrated Christ's death in a larger trinitarian soteriology that gave priority to the activity of God for humanity while also recognizing the incarnate Son's death and resurrection as *empowering* the baptized for *participation* in the divine mystery through the sacraments and their ethical lives. Participation in the mystery of divine love for the life of the world (versus a distant legal act of satisfaction or mere imitation by moral resolve) is the key to the redemption and sanctification of believers. See Gustaf Aulén, *Christus Victor: An Historical Study of the Three Main Types of the Idea of Atonement*, trans. A. G. Hebert (New York: MacMillan, 1977), pp. 1–15, 143–59.

5. Lucien Deiss, *Celebration of the Word*, trans. Lucien Deiss and Jane Burton (Collegeville, MN: Liturgical Press, 1993), p. 21.

6. The Constitution on the Sacred Liturgy: *Sacrosanctum Concilium*, no. 24, accessible at http://www.vatican.va/archive/hist_councils/ii_vatican_council/documents/vat-ii_const_19631204_sacrosanctum-concilium_en.html.

7. See S. Mark Heim, *Saved from Sacrifice: A Theology of the Cross* (Grand Rapids, MI: Eerdmans, 2006); Stephen Finlan, *Problems with Atonement* (Collegeville, MN: Liturgical Press, 2005), and *Options on Atonement in Christian Thought* (Collegeville, MN: Liturgical Press, 2007); David N. Power, *The Sacrifice We Offer: The Tridentine Dogma and Its Reinterpretation* (New York: Crossroad, 1987); Erin Lothes Biviano, *The Paradox of Christian Sacrifice: The Loss of Self, The Gift of Self* (New York: Crossroad, 2007); and

Robert J. Daly, *Sacrifice Unveiled: The True Meaning of Christian Sacrifice* (London/New York: T & T Clark/Continuum, 2009).

8. New Testament and extracanonical metaphors for the fundamental grace that Christ is for humans include adoption, new creation, birth from/being a child of God, gift of the Holy Spirit, being formed in the image of Christ, salvation, redemption, freedom (from slavery), reconciliation, peace/satisfaction, legal deliverance/justification, victory over alienating/demonic power, and more. See Edward Schillebeeckx, *Christ: The Experience of Jesus as Lord*, trans. John Bowden (New York: Crossroad, 1980), pp. 468–511.

9. Daly, *Sacrifice Unveiled*, p. 4.

10. See Powers, *Eucharistic Theology*, pp. 26, 31.

11. New Testament scholar Alan C. Mitchell explains that while the Letter to the Hebrews makes its comparisons with Judaism mostly in terms of ritual and priesthood, "there is nothing really to tie those comparisons to actual Jewish practice at the time Hebrews was written...." *Hebrews*, Sacra Pagina 13, ed. Daniel Harrington (Collegeville, MN: Liturgical Press, 2007), p. 13.

12. Edward Schillebeeckx articulates how Christians tend to get the sacrificial imagery of Hebrews backward: "This philanthropic christology, which works with what in the last resort is a very simple concept of priesthood, is made difficult for us by the complicated comparisons with the Old Testament and Jewish sacrifices for the great day of atonement (Kippur) and the sacrifice connected with the Mosaic tent of meeting. However, for Hebrews what seems to us to be a sacral reinterpretation of the *layman* Jesus in terms of Jewish priesthood is a demythologization of the Jewish image of priesthood. For the author, the love of the human Jesus who suffers for others, in faithfulness to God and in solidarity with the history of human suffering, is priesthood in the true sense of the word: bringing men to God." *Christ*, p. 254.

13. Scott O'Brien, "Partakers of the Divine Sacrifice; Liturgy and the Deification of the Christian Assembly," *Liturgical Ministry* 18 (Spring 2009): 69.

14. Ibid., 76.

15. Barbara E. Reid, "From Sacrifice to Self-Surrender to Love," *Liturgical Ministry* 18 (Spring 2009): 86.

16. Ibid. Reid notes that such early Christian bishops as Ambrose of Milan and medieval mystics as Julian of Norwich capitalized on the birthing imagery in John to describe Christ as the virgin or mother giving birth to us believers.

17. James D. G. Dunn, *Baptism in the Holy Spirit* (London: SCM, 1970), p. 194.

18. Rudolf Schnackenburg, *The Gospel according to St. John*, Vol. 1, trans. Kevin Smyth (New York: Crossroad, 1982), p. 159.

19. Rudolf Schnackenburg, *The Church in the New Testament* (New York: Herder & Herder, 1965), 111. See also, *The Gospel according to St. John*, p. 161.

20. Raymond E. Brown, *New Testament Essays* (Milwaukee: Bruce, 1965), p. 52.

21. Ibid., 95. See also, Raymond E. Brown, *The Gospel according to John I–XII*, The Anchor Bible, Vol. 29 (Garden City: Doubleday, 1966), p. cxiv.

22. C. K. Barrett, *Essays on John* (Philadelphia: Westminster, 1982), pp. 80, 89.

23. Ibid., p. 97.

24. Xavier Léon-Dufour, *Sharing the Eucharistic Bread: The Witness of the New Testament*, trans. Matthew O'Connell (New York: Paulist Press, 1987), pp. 95, 251.

25. Ibid., p. 92.

26. See Schnackenburg, *The Gospel according to St. John*, pp. 396, 161. Recall that even Bultmann recognizes the water and the blood as symbols of the two sacraments, while nonetheless denying the verse's authenticity to the Fourth Gospel.

27. Francis J. Moloney, "Johannine Theology," in *The New Jerome Biblical Commentary*, ed. R. Brown, J. Fitzmyer, and R. Murphy (Englewood Cliffs, NJ: Prentice Hall, 1990), p. 1426.

28. Léon-Dufour, *Sharing the Eucharistic Bread*, p. 252.

29. See ibid., p. 270.

30. See Schillebeeckx, *Christ*, pp. 417–21.

31. See Maxwell E. Johnson, *The Rites of Christian Initiation: Their Evolution and Interpretation*, rev. ed. (Collegeville, MN: Liturgical Press, 2007), pp. xviii, 125, 229, 295.

32. See previous, pp. 7–8.

33. See Bruce T. Morrill, *Anamnesis as Dangerous Memory: Political and Liturgical Theology in Dialogue* (Collegeville, MN: Liturgical Press, 2000), pp. 169–70.

34. See Paul F. Bradshaw, *The Search for the Origins of Christian Worship: Sources and Methods for the Study of Early Liturgy*, rev. ed. (New York: Oxford University Press, 2002), pp. 52–53, 97.

35. See previous, pp. 22–23.

36. Here I follow the brilliant critical summary in Bradshaw, *The Search for the Origins of Christian Worship*, pp. 43–46.

37. Ibid., p. 45.

38. See N. T. Wright, *Jesus and the Victory of God*, Christian Origins and the Question of God, Vol. 2 (Minneapolis: Augsburg Fortress, 1996), pp. 555–59.

39. Ibid., p. 556.

40. See Léon-Dufour, *Sharing the Eucharistic Bread*, p. 110.

41. See David Gregg, *Anamnesis in the Eucharist*, Grove Liturgical Study 5 (Brambcote Notts, UK: Grove, 1976), p. 22.

42. Léon-Dufour, *Sharing the Eucharistic Bread*, p. 111.

43. Wright, *Jesus and the Victory of God*, p. 558.

44. Léon-Dufour, *Sharing the Eucharistic Bread*, p. 58.

45. Ibid., 59. Léon-Dufour cites Psalms 23:5; 16:5; and 116:13.

46. See Mary C. Boys, *Has God Only One Blessing?: Judaism as a Source of Christian Self-Understanding* (New York: Paulist Press, 2000), pp. 75–85, 102.

47. Robert Cabié, *The Eucharist*, The Church at Prayer, ed. A. G. Martimort, trans. Matthew O'Connell, Vol. 2 (Collegeville, MN: Liturgical Press, 1986), 25. Translation of the full text of *Didache*, nos. 9 and 10, the eucharistic material, may be found at pp. 23–24. On the dating of the *Didache* as well as another translation, see Thomas O'Loughlin, *The Didache: A Window on the*

Earliest Christians (Grand Rapids, MI: Baker Academic, 2010), pp. 25–27, 161–71.

48. See Morrill, *Anamnesis as Dangerous Memory*, pp. 197–98.

49. Present author's note: See previous, pp. 23–31.

50. Andrea Bieler and Luise Schottroff, *The Eucharist: Bodies, Bread, and Resurrection* (Minneapolis: Fortress, 2007), pp. 65–66.

51. "Supersessionism, from the Latin, *supersedere* (to sit upon, to preside over), is the theological claim that Christians have replaced the Jews as God's people because the Jews rejected Jesus....Judaism is obsolete, its covenant abrogated." Boys, *Has God Only One Blessing?*, pp. 10–11.

52. In Lawrence J. Johnson, *Worship in the Early Church: An Anthology of Historical Sources* (Collegeville, MN: Liturgical Press, 2009), pp. 67–68.

53. Ibid., p. 68.

54. For Bradshaw's cautions, see *The Search for the Origins of Christian Worship*, pp. 98–99.

55. Cabié, *The Eucharist*, p. 35.

56. See Bradshaw, *The Search for the Origins of Christian Worship*, pp. 136–37.

57. In his catechetical homilies the fourth-century Syrian bishop Theodore of Mopsuestia produced a masterly synthesis of orthodox teaching on the Holy Spirit's role in creation, incarnation, resurrection, and sacraments. See Bruce T. Morrill, "The Many Bodies of Worship: Locating the Spirit's Work," in *Bodies of Worship: Explorations in Theory and Practice*, ed. Bruce T. Morrill (Collegeville, MN: Liturgical Press, 1999), pp. 19–37.

Chapter 4: Leadership for Christ's Body

1. See previous, p. 14.

2. For an overview of current scholarship on the evolution and varied patterns of charismata and offices, see Paul F. Bradshaw, *The Search for the Origins of Christian Worship: Sources and Methods for the Study of Early Liturgy*, rev. ed. (New York: Oxford University

Press, 2002), 194–206; see also his earlier monograph, *Liturgical Presidency in the Early Church*, Grove Liturgical Study 36 (Bramcote, Notts, UK: Grove, 1983).

3. Bernard Cooke and Gary Macy, *Christian Symbol and Ritual: An Introduction* (New York: Oxford University Press, 2005), p. 127.

4. See Edward Yarnold, *The Awe-Inspiring Rites of Initiation: The Origins of the RCIA*, 2nd ed. (Collegeville, MN: Liturgical Press, 1994), pp. 209–10. In addition to Theodore's catecheses, Yarnold provides translations of those by Cyril of Jerusalem, Ambrose of Milan, and John Chrysostom, who all likewise employ the priestly metaphor for the bishop presiding over the rites of initiation, baptism, and Eucharist.

5. John F. Baldovin, "Liturgical Presidency: The Sacramental Question," in *Disciples at the Crossroads: Perspectives on Worship and Church Leadership*, ed. Eleanor Bernstein (Collegeville, MN: Liturgical Press, 1993), p. 36.

6. See Edward Schillebeeckx, *The Church with a Human Face: A New and Expanded Theology of Ministry*, trans. John Bowden (New York: Crossroad, 1988), p. 161.

7. Baldovin, "Liturgical Presidency," p. 36. See also Cooke and Macy, *Christian Symbol and Ritual*, p. 128.

8. See the Dogmatic Constitution on the Church: *Lumen Gentium*, nos. 11, 21, and the Decree on the Ministry and Life of Priests: *Presbyterorum Ordinis*, nos. 4–6, in *Vatican Council II: Vol. I: The Conciliar and Post Conciliar Documents*, rev. ed., ed. Austin Flannery (Northport: Costello, 1996), pp. 362, 372–73, 868–75. See also, Schillebeeckx, *The Church with a Human Face*, p. 203.

9. *Baptism, Eucharist and Ministry*, Faith and Order Paper No. 111 (Geneva: World Council of Churches, 1982), pt. 3, no. 13.

10. See ibid., nos. 6, 34–35, 52–53. Cooke and Macy observe that "few would dispute that central to [the churches and ecclesial communions'] present mutual lack of recognition is the claim of Rome to be the unique leader of Christianity" (*Christian Symbol and Ritual*, pp. 133–35). Pope John Paul II's encyclical, *Ut Unum Sint* (1995), in the present author's opinion, offered a hopeful

word in its proposal that revisiting the office and function of the bishop of Rome in the first millennium is a valid and promising way forward.

11. *Baptism, Eucharist and Ministry*, pt. 3, no. 14.

12. Louis-Marie Chauvet, *The Sacraments: The Word of God at the Mercy of the Body* (Collegeville, MN: Liturgical Press, 2001), p. 48.

13. Ibid., p. 64.

14. Bernard Cooke, "*Sacrosanctum Concilium*: Vatican II Time Bomb," *Horizons* 31:1 (2004): 107.

15. Bernard Cooke, *Ministry to Word and Sacraments: History and Theology* (Philadelphia: Fortress, 1976), p. 645.

16. See previous, pp. 19–23.

17. Nathan Mitchell, *Mission and Ministry: History and Theology in the Sacrament of Order* (Collegeville, MN: Michael Glazier/Liturgical Press, 1982), p. 307.

18. *Baptism, Eucharist and Ministry*, pt. 3, no. 15.

19. See Schillebeeckx, *The Church with a Human Face*, pp. 128, 134; and Cooke, *Ministry to Word and Sacraments*, pp. 35–40.

20. Mitchell, *Mission and Ministry*, p. 308.

21. *Baptism, Eucharist and Ministry*, pt. 3, no. 48.

22. Ibid., pt. 3, no. 34.

23. See Cooke, *Ministry to Word and Sacraments*, p. 208.

24. Cooke and Macy, *Christian Symbol and Ritual*, p. 145.

25. Peter E. Fink, "Spirituality for Liturgical Presiders," in *Disciples at the Crossroads: Perspectives on Worship and Church Leadership*, ed. Eleanor Bernstein (Collegeville, MN: Liturgical Press, 1993), p. 57.

26. See previous, pp. 51–53.

27. The Constitution on the Sacred Liturgy: *Sacrosanctum Concilium*, no. 14, accessible at http://www.vatican.va/archive/hist_councils/ii_vatican_council/documents/vat-ii_const_19631204_sacrosanctum-concilium_en.html.

28. For this paragraph I draw heavily on my previously published work, "Liturgical Music: Bodies Proclaiming and Responding to the Word of God," in *Bodies of Worship: Explorations in Theory and*

Practice, ed. Bruce T. Morrill (Collegeville, MN: Liturgical Press, 1999), pp. 157–72, here especially, p. 168.

29. Aimé G. Martimort, "Structure and Laws of the Liturgical Celebration," in I. H. Dalmais et al., *Principles of the Liturgy*, The Church at Prayer, Vol. 1, ed. A. G. Martimort, trans. Matthew O'Connell (Collegeville, MN: Liturgical Press, 1987), p. 143.

30. See *The Milwaukee Symposia for Church Composers: A Ten Year Report* (Chicago: Liturgy Training Publications, 1992), no. 67.

31. Ibid., nos. 21–22.

Conclusion

1. See Paul McPartlan, *The Eucharist Makes the Church: Henri de Lubac and John Zizioulas in Dialogue* (Edinburgh: T. & T. Clark, 1993); and John D. Zizioulas, *Being as Communion: Studies in the Personhood and the Church* (Crestwood, NY: St. Vladimir's Seminary Press, 1997), pp. 143–69.

2. See David W. Fagerberg, *Theologia Prima: What Is Liturgical Theology?*, 2nd ed. (Chicago: Hillenbrand Books, 2004), pp. 39–45.

3. See Paul Ricoeur, *The Symbolism of Evil*, trans. Emerson Buchanan (Boston: Beacon Press, 1967), pp. 347–53.

4. See Irenaeus of Lyon, *Against Heresies* 5.3.1, in *The Christological Controversy*, trans. and ed. Richard A. Norris Jr., Sources of Early Christian Thought, ed. William G. Rusch (Philadelphia: Fortress, 1980), pp. 59–60.

5. Augustine, Sermon 219, quoted in Sacred Congregation of Rites, *General Norms for the Liturgical Year and the Calendar*, no. 21, in *The Liturgy Documents: A Parish Resource*, Vol. 1, 4th ed. (Chicago: Liturgy Training Publications, 2004), p. 167.

6. The Easter Vigil, no. 10, in *The Sacramentary* (International Commission on English in the Liturgy, 1973).

Index